W9-CSB-102

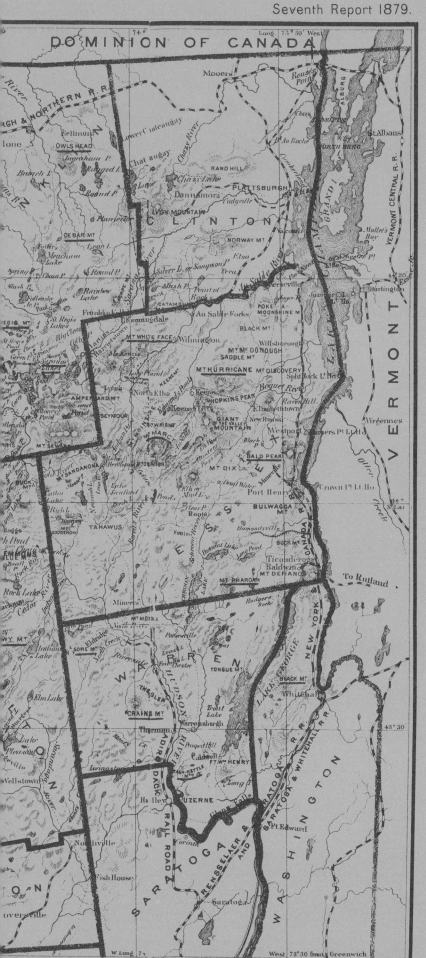

KAMP KOOK'S KIT

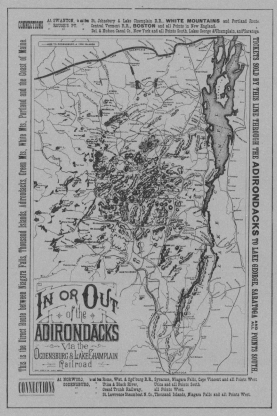

CONNECTIONS

At SWANTON, to and from St. Johnsbury & Lake Champlain R.R., WHITE MOUNTAINS and Portland Route.
" ROUSE'S PT." Central Vermont R.R., BOSTON and all Points in New England.
Del. & Hudson Canal Co., New York and all Points South, Lakes George & Champlain, and Saratoga.

IN OR OUT of the ADIRONDACKS via the OGDENSBURG & LAKE CHAMPLAIN Railroad

This is the Direct Route between Niagara Falls, Thousand Islands, Adirondacks, Green Mts., White Mts., Portland and the Coast of Maine.

TICKETS SOLD BY THIS LINE THROUGH THE ADIRONDACKS TO LAKE GEORGE, SARATOGA AND POINTS SOUTH.

CONNECTIONS

At NORWOOD, to and from Rome, Wat. & Ogd'burg R.R., Syracuse, Niagara Falls, Cape Vincent and all Points West.
OGDENSBURG, " Utica & Black River, Utica and all Points South.
" Grand Trunk Railway, all Points West.
" St. Lawrence Steamboat N. Co., Thousand Islands, Niagara Falls and all Points West.

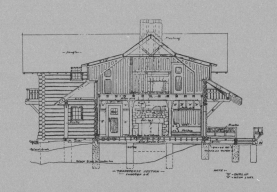

— TRANSVERSE SECTION THROUGH A-B. —

HARVEY H. KAISER

GREAT CAMPS

OF THE

RONDACKS

DAVID R. GODINE

BOSTON

PHOTOGRAPHIC SOURCES
All photographs by the author, except as noted below.

Adirondack Museum
pages 27, 31, 50, 53, 54, 62, 76, 82, 85, 88, 90, 92, 94, 97, 98, 100, 101, 102, 103, 106, 107, 113, 114, 122, 123, 127, 129, 141, 176, 182, 185, 187, 229, 232.

Wareham & Delair
pages 145, 147, 150, 151, 154, 165, 227.

Thomas M. Slade
pages 67, 178, 179, 180.

Richard J. Linke
pages 64, 80, 104, 177, 179, 180, 181.

Paul Malo
page 178.

Seneca Ray Stoddard, from the collection of Jeffrey S. Adler
page vi.

First published in 1982 by
David R. Godine, Publisher, Inc.
Box 450
Jaffrey, New Hampshire 03452

Copyright © 1982 by Harvey H. Kaiser

All rights reserved. No part of this book may be used or reproduced in any manner whatsoever without written permission except in the case of brief quotations embodied in critical articles and reviews.

Library of Congress Cataloging in Publication Data
Kaiser, Harvey H.   1936–
    Great camps of the Adirondacks.

    1. Camp sites, facilities, etc.—New York (State)—
Adirondack mountains—History.   I. Title.
GV198.L3K34   647'.9474753   80-90358

ISBN 1-56792-073-X

Fifth printing, January 1999

Printed in Hong Kong by South China Printing Company

Dedicated to David Hunter McAlpin

CONTENTS

Bog River Falls,
Adirondacks.

ACKNOWLEDGMENTS

Top Ridge Boathouse.

ABOVE ALL, I wish to express my gratitude to the National Endowment for the Arts, whose generous grant in 1978 made the original field research on the Great Camps possible, and to the Educational Facilities Laboratories, whose grant supported the translation of the research into this book. Both programs found it appropriate to award individual grants and their encouragement in awarding fellowships aided me in pursuing a subject that had interested others but had previously eluded pursuit. I am deeply indebted to these organizations for recognizing the project's merits and to their staffs for their support.

Several works by other authors must be acknowledged as key source materials on the people, places, and events surrounding the early history of the Adirondacks and the Great Camps. Harold Hochschild was a leader in preserving the history of the region through his support of the Adirondack Historical Association, the founding of the Adirondack Museum at Blue Mountain Lake, and personal benefactions. His *Township 34* (1952) has been relied upon here as an authoritative source, and permission to quote passages from his book is gratefully acknowledged, along with his personal encouragement for this project. I regret that Harold Hochschild, who died in December, 1980, will not see this book. Alfred Donaldson's *History of the Adirondacks* (1921) provided me many helpful descriptive passages. This two-volume history, written when many personalities of the Great Camp era were available for interviews, remains a basic resource for any research on the Adirondacks. William Chapman White's *Adirondack*

Country (1954) is a tribute to the writer's adopted home. Through his comprehensive and often lyrical story of the North Woods, he has won a place in the hearts of all Adirondackers. The use of passages from his book is gratefully acknowledged.

Many friends, camp owners, and organizations were of help to me in learning the history of the Great Camps, in ferreting out clues to camp locations, and in sustaining the project in its more frustrating moments. Rather than run the risk of offending some whom I may overlook here, I say to all — your assistance has been greatly appreciated. I owe a special debt to several people for their particular encouragement and interest in preserving the cultural heritage of the Great Camps. David Hunter McAlpin of Princeton, New Jersey, has had a lifelong interest in the environmental movement, architecture, photography, and the Adirondacks. He has been a supportive friend throughout the project. His knowledge of the Adirondacks and introductions to camp owners helped move the project forward, often raising sagging spirits with continuous encouragement. The late Marcia Smith, librarian of the Adirondack Museum, was of inestimable value as a source of information, enthusiasm, and comfort. Her knowledge of places and people, her access to information, and her friendship were prime motivating factors in keeping the book on the track. The historian Paul Malo, a colleague at Syracuse University and an early leader in Great Camp preservation, provided guidance and intellectual stimulation throughout the survey and research work. George Crossette and Paul H. Oehser spent many hours reviewing the manuscript in its early stages; their suggestions were most helpful.

A masters' thesis by Mary Ellen Domblewski Gadski at Cornell University, 'The Adirondack Camp of the Last Quarter of the Nineteenth Century,' was an important source in the developing of the research for this book. Its use and assistance are greatly appreciated. While my research was underway, the Preservation League of New York undertook a comprehensive survey of the Great Camps for the New York State Office of Parks and Recreation. The executive director, Diana Waite, shared the League's survey material, along with a report by Mrs. Gadski. The use of their material and the League's encouragement is gratefully acknowledged.

Present and past staff members of the Adirondack Museum have been of great assistance in sharing their time and the Museum's resources. Edward and Sarah Cohen Comstock shared their knowledge of the Camps unselfishly, and their enthusiasm was often inspirational. William K. Verner's scholarship on the subject of the Adirondacks was invaluable, and his editorial comments prevented careless oversights. Tracy Meehan and Vijay Nair aided in archival research.

I am indebted to Professor Richard Linke for the use of his photographs and advice on the project. Maitland DeSormo, founder of Adirondack Yesteryears and prolific writer on the Adirondacks, has also provided photographs and wise counsel on the pursuit of research. I am appreciative of Arthur W. Wareham, architect of Saranac Lake, for the use, from his files, of architectural drawings of work by William Distin and William Coulter.

Of great assistance in the early stages of the research was Vincent Moore, executive director of the Adirondack Park Agency. His personal knowledge of the region provided clues to camp locations and his staff members, George O. Nagle and Richard Jarvis, were of great help. I owe George Fuge, director of the Huntington Outdoor Education Center of the State University of New York at Cortland, located at Raquette Lake, a special debt. His love of the Adirondacks is expressed in the care of the William West Durant's Camp Pine Knot, an example of stewardship of the Great Camp heritage. His personal support in the research and writing of this book is greatly appreciated.

Paul and Jean Soper are two very good friends who lived with this project from its beginning to conclusion, offering company on many expeditions to find camps. Paul's advice on understanding the personalities of the North Woods people was invaluable along with his architectural insights.

I owe a special debt to Syracuse University for the use of Camp Minnowbrook on Blue Mountain Lake and the assistance and encouragement from Chancellor Melvin A. Eggers; Dr. Clifford L. Winters, Jr.; Lucius A. Kempton; and James Moore. Bruce and Mary Darling, now caretakers of Minnowbrook and formerly at Camp Sagamore, showed me the thoughtfulness and consideration I came to recognize as characteristic of many Adirondackers who found their life's work in caring for the Great Camps.

Many people showed me the hospitality of their private camps and shared their reminiscences. At the risk of forgetting a gracious host I list: Mrs. Anna Ordway, Arthur Crocker, and other members of the Tahawus Club; William Witte of Upper Saranac Lake; Lucia Meigs Andrews of Big Wolf Lake; Arthur Savage of the Ausable Club; Samuel B. Webb, Jr., of Nehasane and Shelburne, Vermont; Martha B. Day of Upper Saranac Lake; Jim Bickford of Upper St. Regis Lake; the Edward Litchfields of Litchfield Park; William Rockefeller of Bay Pond Park; Avery Rockefeller of Ampersand Park; Whitelaw Reid of Upper St. Regis Lake; Anthony Garvan of Kamp Kill Kare; Thad and Barbara Collum of the Adirondack League Club; J. Sehl Burns and Holly Burns of The Crows at Keene; Robert and Wilma Evans of Oven Point Camp, Long Lake; Robert Birrell of North Point, Raquette Lake; and Dina Merrill Robertson, formerly of Camp Topridge.

I must note two friends who were helpful in moving the early curiosity about the camps into a 'live' project: Dr. Geraldine E. McArdle aided in formulating the original research, and Matthew Bender IV offered suggestions for publication. Without the patience, encouragement, and assistance of my tolerant secretaries, Andrea Pflug and Helen Cumley, the many drafts would never have been completed.

To my wife Linda and children — Sven-Erik, Robert, and Christina — who shared in many working 'vacations,' my apologies at being perennially distracted, and my thanks for their forbearance of my passion for the Great Camps.

Finally, to David Godine who saw the potential in this subject for publication, my sincerest appreciation. William B. Goodman edited my research into a more readable text, and Frank Lieberman brought an impeccable professionalism to its design.

Although many people contributed to this book in ways both large and small through encouragement, keen interest in the Adirondacks, and a desire to preserve the heritage of the Great Camps, I assume final responsibility for its content.

— HARVEY H. KAISER

The Utowona at the Marion River Carry.

Kamp Kill Kare

*An
Adirondack
Architecture*

THE GREAT CAMPS of the Adirondacks represent a unique epi-
sode in American architectural history. From the end of the
Civil War to the beginning of the Great Depression, a group of
industrialists, financiers, and railroad builders came to northern New
York to build family vacation retreats. The Adirondack mountain region provided them with the opportunity to assemble large private
holdings enclosing lakes, ponds, rivers, and forests set within a region
on the verge of exploitation.

Many of the preserves of lands, the clubs, and the private camps
they built were similar in design and construction. What became
known as the Adirondack Style, characterized by the use of native timber and stone and constructed by locally available labor, emerges in
the rustic designs. The legacy represented by the camps is in jeopardy
today as changing conditions often make owning and maintaining them
too great a burden for the descendants of the builders. As one writer
put the problem, 'The era has passed its zenith.' Concern for preservation of the Great Camps is increasing as they fall into disuse, are altered, or are destroyed.

The central purpose of this book is to inspire action, to propose a
public policy for preserving the Great Camps that still remain. As the
title suggests, this is a book about an architecture set in a special environment. It has three main themes. First, it describes a region of
great natural beauty threatened by speculation, rapacious lumbering,
and, since the mid-1960s, by lethal acid rain. Encompassing an area of
about six million acres — larger than the state of Massachusetts — the

Adirondacks represent one of the last vestiges of wilderness in the United States outside Alaska. Its location, less than a day's travel from the Northeast seaboard's sixty millions, lures tourist traffic bound to damage its precarious environment. It is a region requiring continual vigilance to preserve the health and balance of its natural environment.

The second theme is a celebration of its unique architecture. Toward the end of the nineteenth century, along with the hunters and fishermen who penetrated the wilderness to enjoy the pleasures of the outdoors and the area's abundant fish and game, came the wealthy of the Eastern establishment. They accepted the challenges of the hostile Adirondack environment and built their private retreats, often more complex and extensive than those of Newport or Saratoga. Comfort and luxury coexisted with a vague concept of 'roughing it.' Camps evolved into complexes of unique and elaborate architectural forms. During the relatively short period from 1870 to 1930, Great Camp builders succeeded in creating a style that, although nationally popularized, rarely achieved the elaboration or refinement of these Adirondack prototypes. This vernacular style, with its mixture of logs, native stone, and decorative rustic work of twigs and branches, has been adopted for hotels in the Pacific Cascades, the Rockies, and the Northern Great Lakes, in private vacation homes, and, most notably, in National Park Service buildings across the country.

The third theme presents the conflict between conserving the natural environment and preserving Great Camp architecture. The conflict is typical of a national dilemma arising where distinguished examples of private architecture occur in the remote areas of public park land. The shores of Long Island, the Palisades of the lower Hudson River, and the town of Newport all contain buildings that in time became burdens to their owners and were placed in public trust. The issue is whether architecturally valuable buildings should be retained and restored, or whether they should be removed to return the landscape (insofar as such return is possible) to its natural state. I hope this book will contribute to a comprehensive public policy capable of resolving this question with due consideration to the competing claims.

This book would not have been written if the survival of the Great Camps was not at risk. As with large estates everywhere, changing economic conditions make owning and maintaining private camps financially more and more difficult. The impact of heavier inheritance and property taxes on owners, rising maintenance costs, difficulty in staffing, and the costs of travel and energy have already resulted in the loss of several complexes through deterioration, neglect, or destruction. Other properties are now in jeopardy as owners seek purchasers or alternative uses in order to preserve them intact. A few owners are seeking to negotiate sales to the state of New York, which has already acquired several camps. The state, having protected the natural environment of the Adirondacks for almost a century, must now reassess the terms of this protection if Great Camps reverting to the wilderness preserve are also to be saved from destruction. Such reassessment is complicated by the 'forever wild' provisions of the New York state constitution that have protected the Adirondack Park since 1892.

'The law must be changed or the architecture will be destroyed,' say the architectural preservationists; 'the law must not be changed or the environment will be ruined,' say the environmental conservationists. The question posed by this book is whether the conflict between these equally legitimate claims can be resolved in the public interest. In the competition between opposing positive values, the enlightened person seeks a flexibility that will permit both to flourish.

The impulse to undertake the research for this book took hold during an auction of furnishings at a Great Camp in 1976. Furniture, trophies, and memorabilia were being sold off from Camp Sagamore, a Great Camp begun in 1894 by William West Durant and later expanded by Alfred G. Vanderbilt. Never again, it occurred to me, would it be possible for anyone to experience this camp in its original condition. What about the future of other camps? Would this lamentable dispersal be repeated elsewhere? How many Great Camps were there? Where were they? What was their condition? What were the common denominators, if any, of Great Camps; how were they designed and built? What were the personalities behind them? Asking the questions was easier than finding the answers.

The selection of sites presented in this book is the result of over four years of research. A comprehensive record of the camps does not exist in one single book or research collection. The pieces of the mosaic assembled here were scattered in the works of dozens of authors, the libraries of the Adirondack Museum at Blue Mountain Lake and Saranac Lake Free Library, and the recollections of hundreds of camp owners and Adirondack residents. In some cases, only photographs remain of famous camps; in others, modifications resulting from fires and subsequent 'modernizations' have altered the original structures. Because Great Camp owners sought privacy, they placed their camps in isolated settings, miles from main roads and often accessible only by water. As a result, I traveled over ten thousand miles seeking information on the camps and visiting their sites. The search, requiring car travel, chartered planes and helicopters, boats and guides, canoe journeys, and hiking of miles of trails to find clues to camp locations, took me to the many camps discussed at length in this book.

An extensive search for published work on the Great Camps uncovered only fragmentary articles in contemporary magazines. Alfred

Donaldson's *History of the Adirondacks*, William Chapman White's *Adirondack Country*, and Harold Hochschild's *Township 34* provided the best background material; Augustus Shepard's *Camps in the Woods* helped me to understand the architecture. My inquiries turned up others who shared my deep concern about the camps' future; clearly a movement was already emerging to protect and preserve those camps in greatest jeopardy. It became obvious that if preservation was the ultimate goal, then a methodical survey was a necessary tool. The challenge of the search became its own inspiration and justification.

Capturing the rare quality of the structures on film required permission of the owner, cooperative weather, and suitable lighting. Some camps located deep in woodland shadow or masked by precipitous terrain, defied even my most inspired photographic efforts. It is fortunate indeed that the fine work of nineteenth century photographers like Seneca Ray Stoddard and Edward Bierstadt has been preserved in private collections, for their record of buildings and scenes of early Adirondack recreational development captures the feeling of the times with extraordinary sharpness. Where camps no longer exist, have been drastically altered, or photography was impossible, early photographs from the ground, water, and air have been selected to illustrate camps in their natural environment.

A latticework of logs, intricately joined to provide roof support and create an elegant porch sunscreen.

During the summer of 1976 I conducted the preliminary survey, using the Tahawus Club in the northeast part of the Adirondack Park. I located individuals with extensive personal knowledge of camps, uncovered unpublished research, and contacted organizations with continuing interests in the area. This early work suggested the need for a more comprehensive survey to gather information sufficient for developing a sound public policy that will ensure the future of the Great Camps. Present conservation law is confronted by a problem — architectural preservation — its authors did not foresee. This creates the kind of dilemma it has always been the genius of the American system to resolve.

It is not possible to write in support of the preservation of the Great Camps and their environment without also addressing the century-old local and national conflicts about protection of the natural environment and economic development, and, currently, historic preservation. By presenting an architecture compatible with its environment, an architecture that is extraordinary in its design, and inherent in our national heritage, I frankly hope to ensure the preservation of the Great Camps, as well as to help resolve these apparent national conflicts. There is today an urgent need for social and political innovations that will serve one and all.

CHAPTER
1

THE SETTING

Winter on Blue Mountain Lake — a view from Minnowbrook Lodge

THE ADIRONDACKS are rich in natural beauty, history, and architecture. It is remarkable that after their first sighting by a European, Jacques Cartier, in 1535, three centuries passed before they were mapped and named. In the past hundred years the region, larger than Massachusetts, has changed from a sparsely settled wilderness to one of the nation's most valued recreation areas. Since the founding of the Adirondack Forest Preserve (1885) and the Adirondack Park (1892), the Adirondacks have been seen as what in fact they have become — a living museum of the old wilderness, a sane and sobering reminder of what the land was like before the white men came. Since 1894, two-fifths of the Adirondack Park have been protected by the constitution of the state of New York as a 'forever wild' refuge of unique natural beauty, yet in spite of that constitutional protection, it lies under continual threat of economic exploitation.

The attractive but inhospitable Adirondack terrain — as William Chapman White, its most evocative historian, explains — has been coveted by speculators since the fighting in the eighteenth century 'between French and British and later British and American Rebels for the control of the lake route north and south.' Prior to the colonial wars, its Indian hunting grounds had not been breached by whites; up to that time the region was described as 'a broken, unpracticable tract.' While its spring, summer, and fall were inviting to woodsmen and hunters, its terrain did not tempt farmers hungry for arable land, and its hard, long winters discouraged permanent settlement. Lumbermen harvested its wealth throughout the nineteenth century, and developers of vacation sites have exploited its attractions in the twentieth. Its robust climate, its roaring mountain streams, its lakes, and its heavily pine-bordered ponds have attracted such luminaries as Ralph Waldo Emerson, Robert Louis Stevenson, and Mark Twain, and its natural beauty inspired many of Winslow Homer's best watercolors and oils.

The sixty-year period from the end of the Civil War to the beginning of the Great Depression left a permanent mark on American culture. The industrialists, financiers, and railroad magnates who flourished in these expansive decades amassed incredible wealth. With wealth came a compulsion to spend it, and this they did with a reckless, pre-income-tax abandon. They lived well. Mansions as baronial as any in Berlin or Paris rose along Fifth Avenue in New York; the Metropolitan Museum and the Metropolitan Opera were endowed; travel abroad became more lavish; 'society' in its 'season' became more formal, more avid for occasions. Part of this wealth was, of course, spent in the quest for healthy and wholesome recreation, for escape from the rigors of big business and high society. The Adirondack mountains provided an opportunity to assemble vast private holdings enclosing

1

**The Great
Camps Defined**

the wilderness lakes, ponds, and rivers. The newly wealthy rose to the challenge.

Attracted by the beauty of the region, its healthy atmosphere, and dependable hunting and fishing, they hired local craftsmen to build lodges of native materials on a scale matching the 'cottages' of Newport and the spas of Saratoga. As ownership of an Adirondack lodge became fashionable, the Webbs, Hookers, Vanderbilts, Whitneys, Rockefellers, Harrimans, Lewisohns, and Seligmans built camps in isolated locales surrounded by hundreds of acres. Owners would visit for a few months, weeks, or sometimes only a few days. For the rest of the year the camps — in some cases virtually small villages — were residences for the caretaker staff. Simultaneously, clubs were formed to buy up large tracts of land and create private preserves. These clubs typically may have had a central lodge and private cabins, each member sharing in equal privileges. Private camps built by individuals were similar in design and construction. Collectively called 'the Great Camps,' they reflect a uniform self-sufficiency of structure and intension, mirroring perfectly the men who built them.

Rustic designs compatible to their wilderness environment developed as the regional building style. Consciously sited in remote locations, characterized by the use of logs and indigenous stone, shingled roofs with broad overhangs and porches, and simply-proportioned window and door openings, these building complexes are among our most original examples of vernacular architecture. Although efforts have been made to link their style to European precedents, and particularly to Alpine chalets, the collective work was in fact a logical and inevitable combination of local craft traditions and readily available materials — the Adirondack style.

The Great Camps differed from other recreational developments beyond their use of local craftsmen and materials. Here the goal was a retreat, usually for the entire month of August, sometimes for early spring fishing or late fall hunting. Generally, a Great Camp was a collection of 'rustic buildings,' conveying the character of log constructions in the forest, even if guests dressed formally for dinner and were served with silver and crystal.

In addition to residential quarters, the typical Great Camp was supported by outbuildings designed for the maintenance of the complex and for insulation from the essentially hostile locale and climate. The concept of self-sufficiency incorporated working farms, greenhouses, icehouses, and occasionally even a chapel. Superficially stripped to essentials, the Great Camps were sustained by a complex network of underground water supply, waste collection systems, and eventually electric power lines. It was not at all unusual for the staff to outnumber the guests by three or four to one.

The achievement of Great Camps, as described by Paul Malo was really logistical:

> Probably they were not conceived as means of living simply, despite the calculated appearance of the simple life. More likely, they were undertaken because they were difficult, to prove that it could be done. Difficult in accessibility, difficult to provision, to staff, to maintain. The very difficulty may have motivated the builders, who were rewarded less by public acclaim than by personal satisfaction in taming a hostile environment, and creating a civilized mode of living exclusively by one's own means.

As important as this logistical achievement was the aesthetic accomplishment. An architecture expressing a special approach to natural surroundings was created through deliberate choices in the building site, materials, and the imaginative incorporation of rustic design features. Because the special character of early camp building was quickly recognized as appropriate to the Adirondack environment, a regional style soon developed, although occasionally an Alpine character was affected by adopting the features of Swiss domestic architecture — broad, shallow-sloping roofs with wide eaves, and overhanging upper floors and balconies.

One common feature of most Great Camps was the use of logs as a basic building material. As in other northern, forested regions of the world, logs were readily available and durable, and local traditions provided skill in their use. The wealthy owners who built their Adirondack summer homes to meet exacting standards of luxury and conve-

A cabin in the Adirondacks. From Log Cabins and Cottages, *by William S. Wicks (9th Ed.).*

nience chose logs not only for their accessibility, but also for their particular appropriateness to the natural surroundings. They also fitted in with the romantic notion of the simple life in the unspoiled wilderness. Life in the Great Camps was hardly simple, but elaborate pains were taken to make it seem so.

As a regional architecture, the Adirondack Great Camps have further intrinsic value as examples of successful design and sure craftsmanship. In late-nineteenth-century America, they inspired popular journalists to romanticize about them. Log-building plans were published in 'how-to' books using Adirondack camps as models. The popularity of these places and their suitability to a wilderness setting stimulated similar constructions in the foothills of the Appalachians, the North Woods of the Great Lakes states, and the western slopes of the Rocky Mountains. Later, this same style was translated into the grand lodges at Yellowstone and Glacier parks; it became synonymous with the early architecture of the National Park Service.

The camps depicted in this book have a dual importance: they are tangible and appealing reminders of a vanished life-style, and they are likewise statements about America's early desire to live harmoniously with nature. Taken as a whole, a very strong case can be made for considering them as regional architecture of a very special character and worth. This is an important consideration, for such regional architecture is fast disappearing in our increasingly homogenized culture. A case can and should be made for its appreciation and protection. What better place to begin than with the Great Camps, for in preserving these extraordinary structures, we help hold the past in place and so ensure a precious cultural continuity.

Adirondack Country: Mountains, Lakes, Woods, and Weather

IN *Adirondack Country*, William Chapman White describes a wintertime cottage industry, based not on industrial standards or the guidance of government control, but on goodwill and a desire to revive sweet memories of the Adirondack summer and fall. Balsam needles were dried and stuffed in small pillows to be sent out as presents to those who shared the beauty of the north country. It was as if the fragrant scent of balsam could summon the tranquil beauty of the woods for distant relatives, summer guests, and winter escapees. All that was required was one such redolent gift to recall special memories: the roaring brook, the vista of mountain peaks, the silence of deep woods.

It was the beauty of the area, with its grandeur and wilderness mystique and even its smells and sounds, that attracted men to the area and continued calling them back. First to explore; then to hunt, fish, and trap; to harvest the timber; and finally to settle the region, men came because the woods were a challenge, separating them from their earlier experiences and the outside world. The setting of the Adirondack country, its terrain, climate, and its resources, determined how men built.

The area itself at its southern boundary is only two hundred miles north of New York City and less than fifty miles north of the Erie Canal, which tied Albany to Buffalo along the Mohawk River Valley. Yet it was not thoroughly explored until the 1830s. Lewis and Clark had charted the Northwest Territory to the Pacific three decades before the first ascent of Mount Marcy, the Adirondacks' highest peak. During the 1830s, principally as a result of a statewide natural history survey, the sources of the Hudson River were first explored and the high mountains of northern New York designated 'the Adirondack Group.'

In the days of the colonial settlement of Canada and the Northeast, the area was bypassed because of its ruggedness, lengthy winters, and prohibitively difficult access. Not that the terrain did not intrigue the occasional explorer and the settler; some scattered settlement of the region occurred when Vermonters 'went west' after the Revolutionary War. But when the Erie Canal system provided an easy route to the superior western farm lands, New England's surplus population again bypassed these northern lands and the rugged topography and severe winters continued to thwart settlement for many years. Its greatest attraction was always as an escape. In 1830 the population of the region was 55,000. At the time of early surveying in 1840 the population had reached 70,000. Less than forty years later it was said that the Adirondack country, alive with newly built summer hotels and railroads, was 'hunted out, timbered out, overrun with people, and ruined.' By 1880 the population of the country numbered 113,000 permanent inhabitants. This declined to 89,000 by 1920 and was recorded at 109,000 in 1960. Most of the population is in its score of villages. Still, although sparsely settled, the Adirondacks are within easy reach of sixty million people. How gasoline supplies and transportation costs will affect future settlement is anyone's guess, but the region has in the past adjusted to changing accessibility and probably will continue to do so.

The variety of Adirondack geography is astonishing. One can move from a peak to a valley and from meadow to forest within a few miles. Where one would expect a valley, the glitter of a chain of lakes is often found. However, the terrain, lakes, rivers, and settlements distinguish the region's four distinct quadrants and differences between the quarters have been used to individualize the region ever since the early guidebooks of 1860s and 70s.

The southeast quarter, originally approached from Vermont and Saratoga, has low hills and a few lovely lakes, its eastern edge bordered by an interstate highway. Lake George is at the center of what is largely resort country, and the former line of march for Revolutionary armies now bristles with motels, amusement parks, and fast-food restaurants.

The terrain rises in the northeast quarter to the high-peaks area, all contained within fifty square miles. Across Lake Champlain are the Green Mountains of Vermont, origin of many of the early settlers. This quarter also has the villages of Lake Placid and Saranac Lake, famous for the Winter Olympics and for tuberculosis sanatoria, respectively.

The least-developed quarter of the Adirondacks, the northwest, has had little attraction except in its southernmost part. It contains the village of Tupper Lake and countless lakes, ponds, and rivers. Vast holdings, numbering in the hundreds of thousands of acres, are in the hands of logging companies.

The southwest quarter, characterized by chains of lakes and low hills, is popular for modest second homes of owners from Utica and Syracuse. Here also are the lakes of the early Great Camps, accessible by rail and steamboat, and the villages of Blue Mountain Lake, Long Lake, Inlet, and Old Forge.

Viewed from a mountain top or from the air, the distinctive features of the region become apparent. The high-peaks area runs from the center almost to sea level on all sides. From Lake Champlain to Mount Marcy, less than forty miles, the land rises from one hundred feet above sea level to 5344 feet. In the north, the land levels off into rolling country and broad plateaus.

Calling the Adirondacks 'mountains' may seem hyperbolic to purists familiar with the Alps or the Rockies; the city of Denver, after all, is higher than any Adirondack peak. But elevations in the Adirondacks are deceptive. Even though more than one hundred peaks have elevations higher than 3500 feet, the rounded tops of this ancient range rise above a plateau of 1500 feet or more. The forty-six that are 4000 feet or more represent the 'high peaks.' Centered around the summit of Mount Marcy, they crowd together within fifty square miles. As disordered as the peaks may appear from the ground or air, the axes of five ranges, running from southwest to northeast, are nearly parallel and about eight miles apart. Between their ranges, cross spurs, and eccentric ridges flow the region's rivers, and there the chains of lakes are found.

The region has over 1350 lakes. The largest are Lake George and Lake Champlain, but many others are barely ponds and remain nameless. The highest lake — 4300 feet up on Mount Marcy — is romantically named Tear-of-the-Clouds. It is also the most northerly source of the Hudson. Chains of lakes, inlets, and streams lace the southwest quarter, so interconnecting that canoe trips of one hundred miles, broken only by a few short portages, are possible. The Fulton Chain, Ra-

*Blue Mountain
Lake: 'The Koh-i-noor
of the smaller
wilderness gems.'*

quette, and Long, the three Saranacs, and over forty lakes in the St.
Regis area are linked from southwest to northeast. Small tree-covered
islands dotting some lakes have white sand beaches, but most stay
wooded to the water's edge.

The rivers that thread the mountains and connect the lakes and
ponds are varied. Some are true streams while others are slow 'flows,'
marshy areas that carry the mountain runoff into the larger rivers —
the Raquette, the Saranac, the Oswegatchie, and the Grasse — and
thence into the Hudson and the Saint Lawrence. In the era of early development, the rivers were the highways, carrying logs, steamers, and
the guideboats with hunters and fishermen. Each river system developed its own history, built around its source, the lakes it connected,
and its outlet. Some were lumbermen's rivers, others provided power
through tumbling falls. The Hudson, starting as a pure mountain
stream, ends majestically (if malodorously) at Manhattan. Often called
the American Rhine, it has provided a dramatic tableau for generations of artists who captured its varied moods and conveyed its character, from deep woods to skyscrapers. Its most famous illustrators were
of that considerable group of painters, the Hudson River School,
which included Thomas Cole and Frederick Church.

Mountains, lakes, and rivers mark the region as unusual, but it is
the woods that make the Adirondacks unique. So vast was the original
forest cover that for centuries the area was known simply as the 'North
Woods.' Endless forests of giant spruce and white pine towered above
the maples and birches. Even after years of rapacious timber cutting
and devastating fires, the woods seem imposing, immense, and deeply
impenetrable.

Of the virgin woods the first white man saw, little remains. Intensive commercial lumbering during the nineteenth century and the great fires of 1903 and 1908 took most of them. The New York State Forest Commission estimated that by 1920 less than 4 percent of the forest preserve was virgin timber. This was further reduced by the destructive windstorm of November 25, 1950, which destroyed many of the remaining fine stands. Forest cover today is mostly second growth; in some places it is third and fourth growth.

Mid-nineteenth-century commercial lumbering was so voracious that downstate fears were raised about permanent damage to the watershed. Public pressure moved the state legislature to create the New York State Forest Preserve in 1885, but a compliant governor approved programs condoning continued destruction of the woods. The need to protect the Preserve was so dramatic and obvious that the 'forever wild' amendment was added to the state constitution in 1894.

But let William Chapman White describe the region's most memorable feature:

> The spruces darken as winter comes and gives the hills their black green look, but two other trees add their coloring at other times. Maples fire the hills in autumn, birches set them shining in summer or winter. . . . These and another score of species, from ash to ironwood and balsam, make up the Adirondack woods as they stretch from Poke O'Moonshine in the northeast to the shores of West Canada Creek in the southwest. They clothe the valleys, hills and swamps. They give the land its color, through the greens of spring, the fire reds of autumn, and the blackness of winter.

The very wildness which is the attraction of these natural features has served to protect it from permanent settlement, even in these days of air travel and reduced driving times. A long two-day journey by rail and stagecoach has been shortened to hours, but the minimal network of roads across the ranges and through the deep woods continues to discourage intensive development. Another disheartening feature is the climate. As famous as the north country may be for its beauty, to many it is infamous for its weather. Winters are long and cold; snowfall is deep. Adirondack cold is a dry cold, usually with little wind. Temperatures of $-50°$ F have been recorded in the central Adirondacks. Frosts can occur at any time in summer. Constant drizzle can banish the summer sun for the entire month of August, and every night in July can be chilly enough to make blankets and a fire in the hearth indispensable. Records on Adirondack weather prove just one thing: it is profoundly unpredictable.

And yet the fragrance of a campfire curling through the woods on a September evening, with loons calling across a lake crowded to the shore by tall pines, can create an enchantment that will be remembered for a lifetime.

THERE IS a confusing overlap in the terms Adirondacks, Adirondack Park, and Adirondack Forest Preserve. Because this is a book about the Great Camps of the Adirondacks, camps which occur in locales under all three terms, some clarification may prove helpful.

'The Adirondacks' refers to a mountainous area north of the Mohawk River and provides the general reference for the region. Originally, 'Adirondacks' applied specifically to the great range of mountains that included Mt. Marcy — 'the Adirondack Group,' as named by Ebenezer Emmons early in 1838. When the Adirondack Park was established by law in 1892, the State gave an official boundary to part of the area. A blue line was used on the official map to mark the boundaries: hence the phrases 'inside the Blue Line' and 'outside the Blue Line.' The boundary of the Park was extended eastward in 1931 to encompass all of Lake George and much of the shores of Lake Champlain. The Forest Preserve had been established in 1885 to protect state-owned lands in both the Adirondack and Catskill counties. Confusion fostered by these entities is compounded by the patchwork of ownership by the state in these two upstate New York regions and within the Adirondack Park. Of the six million acres inside the Blue Line, 2,250,000 acres are state lands. The rest is privately owned, with various minor restrictions imposed thereon prior to 1971 and far-reaching land use controls added since then by the Adirondack Park ·Agency. Presently, about one-fourth of the private land is held by the forest products industry. Another third is held by private ownership in parcels larger than 500 acres, including large private estates and clubs.

Thus we have a New York State Forest Preserve, consisting of lands owned by the state in twelve Adirondack and four Catskill counties, and dating back to 1885. In 1894 the effectiveness of the Forest Preserve protection was significantly strengthened by amendments to the state constitution. In 1892 the Adirondack Park, encompassing major portions of the Forest Preserve along with considerable areas of private land, was established by law. These successive actions were instigated by citizens increasingly distrustful of the administrative and legislative controls over the region. The ultimate expression of their concern was the incorporation into the state constitution, in 1894, of amendments providing that public ownership may not 'be leased, sold, or exchanged, nor shall the timber thereon be sold, removed, or destroyed.' Not only shall 'the Forest preserve . . . be forever kept as

The
Adirondack
Park

wild forestland,' but the character of the public lands may not be altered, except by constitutional amendment, voted on by all citizens of the state. 'Forever wild' means that relatively little in the way of timber cutting or conventional forest management is to be permitted on State land. It also means that any structures, including Great Camps, cannot continue to exist if acquired on land incorporated into the Preserve. Thus the dilemma between preservation of either environment or architecture becomes a potential constitutional issue.

The Blue Line boundary defines a space of 120 miles on four sides, enclosing an area of 9375 square miles. Inside the Blue Line of the Adirondack Park are all or part of twelve counties: all of Hamilton and Essex counties, half of Franklin, a large part of St. Lawrence, Herkimer and Warren, and small parts of Lewis, Fulton, Saratoga, Clinton, Washington, and Oneida counties.

The Park as it now exists is larger than any other of the 2000 state forests and parks in the United States. Only the Alaska National Park formed by the Alaska lands bill of December, 1980, is larger. None has the unique pattern of development of private land alongside public land. The fact that the Adirondack country has been a state park since 1892 and that two-fifths of it is protected by the constitution keeps the woods wild and thereby gives the Adirondacks their greatest appeal.

The Environment's Influences on Architecture

GEOGRAPHY, available building materials, weather, and the history of settlement influence the development of a regional style of architecture. Where settlers came from is a clue to the styles and construction techniques that, over time, become indigenous to an area. Local skills emerge gradually as early building traditions adapt to limitations peculiar to a region. In the Adirondacks the rugged terrain, an almost inexhaustible supply of timber, and owners' desires shaped the style and construction of the Great Camps.

Early Adirondack settlers cleared the land and used the felled logs to build cabins as temporary shelter. A fancy cabin, such as the Adsit's built at Westport in 1778, might be twenty-four feet long and eighteen feet wide. A crude settler's cabin would have an earth floor, a blanket hung over an opening for a doorway, and greased paper covering the few window openings. A stone fireplace would be a fancy touch; more commonly a fire would be built on the ground at the end of the cabin, leaving the smoke to wander up through a hole in the roof. Weather was sealed out of chinks between the logs by cedar wedges on the inside and moss and clay on the outside. However, as soon as the first water-driven mills were built, settlers usually erected frame houses for permanent use.

As Revolutionary War soldiers migrated westward from Massachusetts, Connecticut, and Vermont, and north up the Hudson from New York, contemporary colonial domestic designs were introduced to the region. Books like Pain's *Practical House Carpenter* (1796), and Asher Benjamin's *The Country Builder's Assistant* (1796) and *American Builder's Companion* (1806), inspired plans and stylistic details still to be seen in the Lake Champlain and Mohawk Valley areas. The homes, churches, and stagecoach inns of the early 1800s were of dimensioned lumber, clapboard and Georgian in detail. As with most 'colonial' periods of architecture, the refined style of the early Republic did not suit the region's needs. Soon roof pitches were flattened to hold the heavy snow as insulation against the wind and cold; openings for doors and windows were reduced in size to minimize heat loss and the use of hard-to-come-by window glass. To provide shelter during the long periods of rain and snow, eaves were extended and porches added.

The indigenous architecture of the Adirondacks, with its roots in northern New England, stressed wood frame construction. The sophisticated camp builders, such as Durant, created an 'Adirondack Style' and harnessed local talent to build to their romantic specifications. Not surprisingly, building construction and styles in the Adirondacks evolved along lines similar to those of domestic architecture in timbered northern regions elsewhere in the world. Viollet-le-Duc describes these vernacular log and native stone styles as they are found in Alpine and Scandinavian Europe, northern Russia, and Japan, and resembling in many ways Adirondack-style cabins. Just as in the Adirondacks, these are all of wood. The size and form of a building are

The Adsit Cabin, built at Willsboro Point in 1778.

11

Views from Viollet-Le-Duc's Habitations of Man *(1876). Left, view of Scandinavian House; right, Himalayan dwelling.*

influenced by the limitations of material and its responses to weather. Stone foundations protect timbers from ground dampness; notched corners strengthen walls; and wide overhangs throw rain and snow away from foundation and walls. In the Adirondacks, logs cut from the surrounding woods provided timber for structure, and the readily available granite became foundations and chimneys. Trimmed planks finished the interior and were shaped into furniture by the skilled woodsmen. Wrought iron from local forges provided the hardware. Only glass and 'elegant' trimmings had to be hauled in by stagecoach or wagon.

The rough skills of early settlers were soon improved by the immigrants who came to the Adirondacks to work in the new industries of logging and mining. Swedes, Finns, and central Europeans showed their skills in joinery and ironwork, and their native traditions of building began to merge into the Adirondack style. Hotel builders of the mid-nineteenth century eagerly sought the best talents and hired them away from one another, only to be outbid later by the Great Camp owners. The Adirondack guide who had to survive by his skills year-round became a jack of all trades who could find the best fishing spot, track down deer, and lay up a stone chimney.

The terrain and weather also influenced the selection of sites and orientation of the earliest buildings. Long winters and brief summers dictated sites that could be reached from main 'roads,' actually rough trails. Rivers and lakes served as highways, and locations accessible by the shortest overland hauls were favored. Teams of oxen were used to bring materials over mountains and sometimes over frozen lakes. A dramatic site was seldom foremost in the minds of the settlers because it usually was just too difficult to reach. When Anthony Garvan points out that the basic intention of the Great Camp was to achieve the 'improbable if not the impossible,' he illustrates the contrast between the log cabins of the early settlers and the rustic hunting lodges of the rich.

Heavy snowfalls that covered the ground for almost half the year, and extended spring and summer wet periods, eventually dictated the construction of connections between units and determined other building forms and structural details. On a dry summer's day it is difficult to conceive of the precautions necessary to protect one against the capricious local weather. Rains lasting for weeks, or blizzards dropping out of a sunny fall afternoon, are typical of the Adirondacks' unpredictable ways. Generations of experience taught builders to use oversize timbers to support roofs that had to carry over ten feet of drifted snow. Roofs, extending far beyond exterior walls, precluded a buildup of ice and snow pressure against foundation walls. Logs were flattened and joined tightly, then chinked with caulking of hemp or plaster to keep out the wind-driven rain and cold. A knowledgeable builder raised all logs off the ground onto stones to prevent dampness and rot, and metal shields were used to discourage carpenter ants.

Dread of swift-spreading fire inspired other features that became part of the Adirondack style. To prevent sparks from a chimney landing on a dry roof, stonework was raised well above a roof ridge; stone caps, placed on short corner posts of a chimney, trapped the sparks. This unique device became a typical detail. Smaller single-purpose structures were often separated from each other, to prevent the spread of fire; these were then connected by covered passages. A campsite could take on the appearance of a small village with individual buildings for sleeping, dining, and so forth. This practice, first instituted by early vacationers using tents on platforms, was later translated into permanent log buildings.

The aesthetic virtue of the Adirondack style lies in the deft combination of subtle but pragmatic details that both protect a building against the elements and harmonize with the environment. Buildings grew to 'fit,' gradually acquiring a patina that matched the surrounding landscape. A dash of color, usually red, seen on window frames, provides an occasional contrast to the neutral, natural materials. As at Sagamore, this red may indeed be of a very natural and local source, such as the so-called 'Johnsburg red' from North Creek. It was probably this adroit blending of surroundings and forms that caused the journalists of the late nineteenth century to call the early vacation retreats 'artistic.'

The Adirondack Style

13

CHAPTER
2

OPENING THE ADIRONDACKS

The Adirondacks, across Lake Champlain, from Vermont.

EFORE THE LAND was broken up for private camps, before the hotels and railroads were built, even before the first hardy settlers started West with the 'New York fever,' the vast, unmapped wilderness of northern New York State was virtually uninhabited, for even the Indians chose less rugged terrains for their settlements. The history of permanent settlements in the area starts less than four hundred years ago. About the earliest inhabitants, the Indians, facts are few.

Champlain reported an encounter with Iroquois, on the lake that was subsequently to bear his name, in 1609:

> Now we travelled only by night and rested by day. . . .
>
> At nightfall we embarked in our canoes to continue our journey and as we advanced very softly and noiselessly, we encountered a war party of Iroquois, about 10 o'clock at night at a point west of a cape which juts into the lake on the west side. . . .
>
> Our savages killed several of them and took ten or twelve prisoners. The rest carried off the wounded. Fifteen or sixteen of ours were wounded by arrows. . . .
>
> Having feasted, danced, and sung, we returned three hours afterward, with the prisoners.

Early claimants to the region were two hostile tribes: the Mohawks (called Iroquois by the French), one of the Five Nations in central New York; and the Algonquins, a Canadian tribe. They visited the area from time to time for hunting and trapping, but lands more arable were available in the broad valleys on all sides of the mountains for the relatively small number of Indians.

Later, Jesuit missionary work among the Indians brought white men into the Adirondack region or around its edges. Between 1657 and 1769 there were twenty-four missionaries among the Mohawks. Little is recorded of their success; tales of their capture and murder suggest a mixed reception at best. The enormous demand for beaver hats in Europe sent French, Dutch, and Indian trappers to the periphery of the region on a less dedicated but far more profitable mission. By the mid-seventeenth century, skins were being traded and shipped from Montreal and Albany by the thousands. The pushing and shoving between the French in the north and the English in the south over control of the rich fur trade through the Lake Champlain–Lake George valley was inevitable. Years of war followed, with Indians allied on each side. The war was finally settled in 1759, and the Indians were as much the losers as any settlers on the wrong side of the British victors.

The wars had drawn attention to the area. As far away as the drawing rooms of Boston and New York, land speculators saw opportunities to acquire large tracts of timber-covered land at low prices. In 1776, Thomas Pownall, Royal Governor of Massachusetts, had conceded the Adirondacks as a hunting ground of the Indians, admitting the Europeans' ignorance of the region he called 'The Dismal Wilderness or Habitation of Winter.' This gesture, for it was little more than that, certainly gave the impression that the Indians would be allowed to keep this space for themselves. But, although the unclaimed lands of the state thus belonged to the Indians, the British Crown shrewdly required Indian title to pass first to white men before claims could be staked. Each change of hands gave the Crown a chance to collect large fees for its services.

In 1771, two Manhattan shipwrights, Joseph Totten and Stephen Crossfield, asked for the right to purchase a large triangle of land in the central Adirondacks, a major transaction that was to shape later land deals in the region. Acting only as front men, the two shipwrights were protecting speculators from political enemies who might block the deal. The Mohawks agreed to sell the land for 1135 pounds, about four acres for a penny. (The tract was estimated to contain 800,000 acres, although modern estimates place it at closer to 1,115,000 acres.) The Crown's fee for negotiating the transfer of title was forty thousand pounds — eight times the Indians' asking price. Later, when the Revolution began, the deal evaporated and the entire tract reverted to the people of New York, but the Totten and Crossfield purchase had another singular importance. Planning to subdivide the land into fifty townships and sell it at a profit, the new purchasers, represented by Totten and Crossfield, ordered a survey led by Archibald Campbell. Campbell's crew not only produced the first survey of the area, but traveled a large part of previously unexplored land as well.

When the war ended, the land speculators returned to the region, along with war veterans who had fought on its fringes and remembered the endless forests and the empty land. A small trickle of original settlers returned to the Champlain Valley, but newcomers arrived, struck by a strange malady known as the 'New York fever.' As described by William Chapman White,

> It hit all of New England, but particularly Vermont. It was spread by returned soldiers who had fought on the shores of Lake Champlain and fired by occasional trappers who had ventured into the woods beyond those shores. One man told another that there, to the west, was fine land free for settling; to New England people in 1783, and particularly to Vermont people, the Adirondack country across Lake Champlain was 'the West.' The New York fever struck especially at younger sons of large families or at men who had no luck and saw no future on New England

land. That the land they moved to was little better than the land they left, and rockier, didn't bother them; for the moment it was free, and theirs for the taking.

The Adirondacks also captured the attention of Manhattan land speculators. After the Revolution, the federal government and every state all had unclaimed lands and competed for buyers; thus the Adirondack land deals had nothing unusual about them except their size. In order to repay its Revolutionary War debt, New York State moved to sell its state lands; the first buyer was Crossfield, who confirmed his earlier purchase at the increased price of twelve cents an acre. The land was subdivided, with the largest purchaser the son of an Irish immigrant, Alexander Macomb, a New Yorker who had grown rich in the fur trade on the frontier at Detroit. In 1791, with state land commissioners authorized to sell 'the waste and unappropriated lands of the State,' Macomb came forward. He made an offer for all the Adirondacks area outside of Totten and Crossfield's purchase, extending north to the St. Lawrence River and west to Lake Ontario — a total of 3,816,960 acres. His offer of eight pence an acre — sixteen cents — was accepted, but his ownership was short-lived. Three months after its completion, following the failure of a scheme to sell shares in a new bank, Macomb was bankrupt and in debtors' prison. After 1792, 'Macomb Purchase' lands were divided many times again. Macomb was one of a group of Irish-Americans who speculated and settled in the Adirondacks. They left a legacy of Irish place names, including Clare, Killarney, Tipperary, Moira, Bangor, and St. Patrick.

Speculation in Adirondack lands continued for the first thirty years of the nineteenth century, including ingenious sales to Dutch and French land-development companies, but land values and interest in the region slowly declined as better agricultural land opened in the West. In time, land that speculators could not sell reverted to the state for unpaid taxes. Until 1883 the state was willing to sell its land to any buyer, although in that year it withdrew its remaining holdings from further sale. When the Forest Preserve was organized in 1885, the state's ownership amounted to only 720,744 of the region's 5,000,000 acres.

IN THE post-Revolutionary years a sprinkling of small settlements developed in the valleys surrounding the Adirondacks. The villages of Elizabethtown, Westport, Keesville, and others gathered near the shores of Lake Champlain; on the flatlands to the north and west were similar small villages — Malone, Gouverneur, Canton, and Boonville. The woods remained uninhabited, but for the occasional isolated settlers who somehow managed to survive.

The Post-Revolutionary Years

17

The trackless woods were eventually crossed by trails between set-tlements, the paths marked by blazed trees; these were gradually re-placed by primitive roads. In Alfred Donaldson's words, 'They were passable enough in summer but impassable in spring and impossible in winter.' Better roads were eventually built in the flat land around the mountains, and by 1820 a well-developed road system was being used by coaches and lumber wagons. Sporadic attempts at settlement oc-curred in the interior of the woods as more enterprising settlers built grist mills and sawmills by streams. Lumbermen based their operations near their mills, and villages grew. But the weather and the rugged terrain were discouraging, and settlers would clear one place only to sell it and move on to another. Those that remained drifted into other activities to supplement their incomes — hunting and fishing, working for the lumbermen in winter, working in those mines that existed nearby.

Tilling the land did not interest the New Englander heading for 'the West'; it was the riches growing out of the ground — the forests — that sparked the opening of the wilderness. To the early settlers the supply of timber was so abundant that it appeared inexhaustible. As the tim-ber was cut back from the shores of Lake Champlain and further from the sawmills, the mills had either to close down or move deeper into the woods. The need for transportation to and from the remote mill sites mandated improved roadbuilding. Inns to serve the lumber team-sters soon appeared along the roads. Driving the cut softwoods by road became more difficult, and enterprising lumbermen cut the 200-foot-high white pines into 13-foot lengths, floating single logs to mill on tur-bulent spring streams. As early as 1813, a pair of ingenious brothers, Norman and Alanson Fox, began winter logging, using oxen to haul the timber over iced roads to a river and thence floating it to a mill. Ac-cess to stands of trees in remote areas was made possible by building temporary dams on streams, the log-cut piled below. When the spring thaw came and streams flowed, the dam was knocked out, sending the winter cut to the mills. Gradually the lumbermen moved inland. Among the early loggers were the French Canadians, who proved to be the best of the lumbermen. In another generation, immigrants from Scandinavia joined the logging teams.

Lumber companies bought land by the thousands of acres; when they had removed the big trees, they let the land revert to the state for taxes. By 1850, lumbermen reached the center of the Adirondacks, and New York was producing more lumber than any state in the Union. The state's cut that year was more than a half million trees yielding over a billion board feet. The industry declined as the soft-woods were cut over, only to return and reach a peak in 1905 as chemi-cal processes for converting hardwoods to wood pulp made their har-

Left, *an Adirondack lumber camp at the turn of the century housed between fifteen and forty-five men, a woman cook, and a helper. The typical camp had a main building with two large first-floor rooms, one for cooking and dining, and the other the men's common room. Sleeping quarters were in an attic loft with tiered bunks. Below,* after a day's logging at an Adirondack lumber camp.*

vesting profitable. Uncut forests, fortunately now protected as 'forever wild,' tempt the lumber industry today as they did two hundred years ago.

Tales of the riches above ground are matched by what men found below it. Iron ore was discovered in black sand on some of the lake shores, in hard rock close to the surface and in harder rock buried deep. The first man to discover Adirondack iron is unknown, but early Champlain valley settlers were aware of rich deposits. Conversion of the iron ore was facilitated by the readily available water power. The first settlement at what is now Lake Placid was a small forge. A settler could become an ironmaker by using a simple firebox to hold the ore, converting timber at hand into charcoal for fuel, and using water power to turn a wheel to break down the residue of slag and metal.

New York investors, attracted by the news of ore, hired men to search the region. Attractive ore beds were discovered in the Champlain valley and Adirondacks. The spread of inexpensive forges took its toll of the forest: to make one ton of metal from four tons of ore took six hundred bushels of charcoal. But the riches rarely materialized in the central Adirondacks. Impurities in the ore made it hard to work, and ironmakers complained that the quality of the finished iron varied widely. Considering the efforts, rewards were meager and unreliable except in the Champlain valley, and dreams of wealth soon evaporated.

One of the great romantic stories of the Adirondacks surrounds the discovery of the McIntyre ore beds north of Newcomb, at Tahawus. Both White and Hochschild report the tale at length. A friend, and later son-in-law, of Archibald McIntyre, one David Henderson, was exploring the woods in 1826 for iron deposits. Henderson reported that 'a strapping young Indian of a Canadian tribe made his appearance, the first in the settlement for three years. The Indian opened his blanket and took out a small piece of iron ore, saying, "You want to see 'em ore? Me find plenty — all same." ' For one dollar and a plug of tobacco he would lead them to a rich vein. The Indian led Henderson's party south from near Lake Placid through Indian Pass to the head of Lake Sanford and an obviously rich and apparently pure ledge of iron ore five feet high and fifty feet broad, surrounded by vast deposits. Placing the Indian under guard, the party raced for Albany to buy the land.

The mines at Tahawus were worked for thirty years, despite cholera epidemics, floods, inadequate water supply, and inexperienced labor. Although the ore made excellent iron, its impurities made it slow to work and thus not altogether competitive. By 1857 the mine was closed, its thriving village abandoned; the site became a curious relic for tourists. Eventually, the 'impurities' provided a happy ending to the story. It was titanium, a valuable source for white pigment, and a source for metal alloys in World War II. The site is now owned and actively mined by the National Lead Industries.

Of the more than two hundred Adirondack iron mines and forges worked during the nineteenth century, only two have been continuously successful — the rich deposits at Mineville, behind Port Henry on Lake Champlain, and at Star Lake, St. Lawrence County. The shafts at Mineville provided iron ore for cannonballs used by Benedict Arnold in his naval engagement with the British, and went into the steel that sheathed the *Monitor* in the Civil War. Some mines are still worked today, but their greatest contribution was not the wealth they generated but the notice they brought to the region.

The tremendous supplies of lumber and iron made it clear to settlers and speculators that the Adirondack country could be made prosperous if it could be made accessible. Its mountain scenery kindled interest in tourism. Efforts were made to improve roads, to build canals and railroads to transport the log and metal harvest, and to accommodate the tourist. Albany took note of the growing demand, and the legislature decided to find out about the great wilderness as well as other parts of the state. In 1836, Governor William L. Marcy appointed Ebenezer Emmons, a professor of Williams College, to survey the Adirondacks and report to the legislature. The wilderness was about to be opened.

FROM THE MIDDLE of the 1830s until the end of the Civil War in 1865, the Adirondack region became a special part of the northeastern cultural scene. William K. Verner has called this period the 'Golden Years' of the Adirondacks. It was the period that hung in the balance between public knowledge and the ultimate opening of the wilderness. An island of wildness in a rapidly industrializing part of the country, it inspired an extraordinary body of writing and art. Despite the reality of the Industrial Revolution, the dominant flavor of the age remained recreational and romantic. The 'picturesque' was a major conceit of mid-nineteenth-century American sensibility, and the Adirondacks were perfect for it.

Reports of Emmons's exploration in 1837 began to attract the curious with rifles, fishing gear, and notebooks and sketchbooks in hand. A trickle of articles, started by William C. Redfield, who accompanied Emmons, soon grew into a steady stream of stories about Adirondack travel and adventure. One early 'discoverer' was Charles Fenno Hoffman, a writer and editor for the popular magazine *The New York Mirror*. Hoffman had become a wilderness enthusiast on his earlier travels through the Mississippi Valley; his *A Writer in the West*, published in 1835, extolled the 'singular joyousness in a wilderness.' Within weeks

Opening the Wilderness

of the newspaper accounts of the first ascent of Mt. Marcy, on August 5, 1837, he left for the north country. In 1839, he published a collection of articles, *Wild Scenes in the Forests,* that set a pattern for later Adirondacks books and anticipated the region's future popularity.

Joel Headley's *The Adirondac; or Life in the Woods* also went through many successive editions from 1849 through 1875. Extolling the benefits of vacations in the woods, Headley was an early reporter of the bountiful supply of fish and game for the sportsman, as well as of the curative properties of pine-scented mountain air. He assured his readers of the 'enchantment' in finding in the wilderness escape from 'the strifes of men and the discords of life.' As for himself: 'I love the freedom of the wilderness and the absence of conventional forms there. I love the long stretch through the forest on foot, and the thrilling, glorious prospect from some hoary mountain top. I love it, and I know it is better for me than the thronged city, aye, better for the soul and body both.' Headley concluded his book with 'Directions to the Traveler.' Equipped with strong legs, a stout heart, and a 'love for the wild, and free,' anyone could enjoy an Adirondack vacation 'and come back to civilized life a healthier and better man.'

While Hoffman and Headley described the attractions of the region to a growing band of outdoor enthusiasts, an Albany journalist, Samuel H. Hammond, became one of the first to speak of the conflict between wilderness preservation and utilitarian demands. In his *Wild Northern Scenes; or Sporting Adventures with the Rifle and the Rod* (1857), Hammond discussed the relative virtues of wilderness and civilization under the guise of a dialogue among members of his camping party. Preservation of limited wild areas resolved the dilemma. Describing his plan, Hammond declared he would 'mark out a circle of a hundred miles in diameter, and throw around it the protecting aegis of the constitution. I would make it a forest forever in which the old woods should stand here always as God made them.' Lumbering or settling would be prohibited. Wilderness was to be maintained, although Hammond immediately reassured the reader that civilization would not suffer. His circle of primitive forest, while insuring the continued existence of some wild country, would hardly inhibit development outside the circle. 'There is room enough for civilization in regions better fitted for it. It has no business among these mountains, these rivers and lakes, these gigantic boulders, these tangled valleys and dark mountain gorges. Let it go where labor will garner a richer harvest, and industry reap a better reward for its toil.' In this way, Hammond first set forth the concept of 'forever wild,' a region protected by the constitution of the state. While the romantic writing of others bypassed the problem of protecting the wilderness, Hammond proposed the actions that were recognized as essential forty years later.

The Wilderness Escape

A Circle of a Hundred Miles

Many more collections of hunting and fishing tales appeared in print during the next twenty years. The books sold well and were widely read. One of the more delightful accounts was written by a lady-in-waiting to Queen Victoria, the Honorable Amelia Matilda Murray, on a trip in 1856 with a party that included Governor Horatio Seymour. She sallied forth from Elizabethtown, armed with tea, biscuits, lemons, portable soup, and arrowroot. The first leg of the journey, on buckboard and wagon, was too civilized for the lady. She looked forward with excitement to travel by boat and on foot, hoping 'to travel more than a hundred miles with packs on our backs and staffs in our hands — this will be delightful.' Out of the wilderness at last, at Utica, she reported, 'Three days were necessary to recruit and repose myself.'

Artists reinforced the written word in making the wilderness attractive to city-dwellers. Landscape painters Thomas Cole, Asher B. Durand, and Sanford Gifford were among the first to paint the mountains and were followed by some of the century's most prominent artists. Arthur Fitzwilliam Tait celebrated the call of the hunt in Adirondack settings, and his scenes of masculine adventure in the woods were frequently lithographed for popular Currier and Ives prints of the 1850s and 1860s. The encampment that has come to be known as the Philosopher's Camp, inspired by the back-to-nature works of both lit-

Adirondack hunters

erature and painting, was characteristic of the times. A group presided over by Ralph Waldo Emerson and including James Russell Lowell, Louis Agassiz, and others, chose Follensby Pond in the central Adirondacks as a temporary campsite in 1858. William James Stillman's famous painting, and Emerson's own tribute to the region published in a book of verse in 1860, made the camp legendary, and gave credence to the novel idea of camping in the woods. Providing lodging and access for the travelers to the 'newly discovered' area presented opportunities to the handyman and speculator alike. Settler families found a livelihood in offering shelter to sportsmen and tourists en route to their camps. Ever ingenious at survival, many a settler or lone hunter found he could get paid for doing the very thing he liked best, and the Adirondack guide was born.

An Early Railroad Scheme

As early as 1834 schemes had been concocted to build railroads into the Adirondacks. Routes were surveyed and prospectuses issued, but the investors rarely saw any building. In 1857 the Sackett's Harbor and Saratoga Railroad Company, reorganized as the Lake Ontario and Hudson River Railroad Company, received a state charter and planned to build from Saratoga westward through the central Adirondacks to Sackett's Harbor, on Lake Ontario beyond Watertown. It purchased 250,000 acres of state land at six cents an acre and managed to attract the attention of British investors. But like its predecessors, the project foundered, this time with the outbreak of the Civil War. The region was to see little in the way of railroad tracks until the 1870s.

As the Civil War drew to a close, the lure of the wilderness spread. War meant prosperity for some, including opportunities for summer vacations. Saratoga was abandoned by the Southern planters and their families who had summered there before the war, but were now too poor to return. In their place came northerners newly rich. The small stream of tourists into the Adirondacks continued to rise, but with that rise came alarms over consequent changes: changes in the way people were coming into the woods and changes in the woods themselves.

The new popularity of the region focused attention on the disappearance of its wilderness qualities. Lumbermen at work in the 1850s were still interested in the bigger trees, of course, but did not have the slightest notion of conservation. The acreage they cut denuded many a hillside; there were stretches of the mountains that had been lovely in the 1850s but displayed only water-soaked stumps thirty years later. Lakes and rivers had been drained by lumbermen for their drives, or diverted by steamboat operators. To most people of the time, an unspoiled landscape constituted a tempting invitation to exploitation. Any other attitude was inimical to progress. When the conservation movement did arise in America in the 1870s, it was strengthened by a growing urgency to save the Adirondacks.

Two events occurred in 1864 presaging the end of the 'Golden Years' in the Adirondacks. On August 9, the *New York Times* published an editorial offhandedly acknowledging the conflict between preservation and industrial progress. That editorial, an early recognition by a metropolitan newspaper of the need to 'save the woods,' said in part:

> Within an easy day's ride of our great city as steam teaches us to measure distance, is a tract of country fitted to make a Central Park for the world. . . . it embraces a variety of mountain scenery, unsurpassed, if even equaled, by any region of similar size in the world; . . . its lakes count by hundreds, fed by cool springs, and connected mainly by watery threads, which make them a network such as Switzerland might strive in vain to match; and . . . it affords facilities for hunting and fishing, which our democratic sovereign-citizen could not afford to exchange for the preserves of the mightiest crowned monarch of Christendom. . . .
>
> The furnaces of our capitalists will line its valleys and create new fortunes to swell the aggregate of our wealth, while the hunting-lodges of our citizens will adorn its more remote mountain sides and the wooded islands of its delightful lakes. . . .
>
> In spite of all the din and dust of furnaces and foundries, the Adirondacks, thus husbanded, will furnish abundant seclusion for all time to come: and will admirably realize the true union which should always exist between utility and enjoyment.

The second event was unheralded but far-reaching. In the summer of 1864 a young Connecticut clergyman visited the Adirondacks on a fishing trip; his name was the Reverend William Henry Harrison Murray, and that trip changed the course of many lives.

WHEN MURRAY ACCEPTED the post of pastor of the Park Street Congregational Church of Boston in 1868 he was only twenty-eight, but notes on his Adirondack experiences had already been published by a Connecticut newspaper. The Yale graduate seemed settled for a career in the ministry until his Adirondack sketches were collected in book form in April 1869. No simple statement did more to publicize the region than Murray's *Adventures in the Wilderness; or Camp-Life in the Adirondacks.*

It may have been the timing of its appearance — the nation's war-weariness was being replaced by a growing prosperity and a new sense

The Rush Is On

of adventure. Whatever the reasons, Murray's *Adventures* was immensely successful. Donaldson reports that it displaced the popular novel of the day: 'Everybody seemed to be reading it, and a great many people were simultaneously seized with the desire to visit the region it described.' Within months after publication there was a stampede to the woods. The influx was known as 'Murray's Rush,' and those who came with extravagant ideas of comfort and excitement found that they were called 'Murray's Fools.'

In reading the book today, it is difficult to understand why it should have had such an effect. Perhaps the book was lent credence for having been written by one of Boston's most distinguished clergymen. For thirty years prior to its appearance, at least ten books of travel and adventure in the Adirondacks had appeared. Hoffman, Headley, and other writers had attracted sportsmen to the region with earlier descriptions of the forests and streams teeming with game and fish. But Murray's book was clearly different. With its specific details on costs, routes, hotels and guides, and proper clothes and provisions, it was an enticing Adirondack guidebook. And beyond its practicality, it gave the author's personal reasons for seeking the wilderness.

For a clergyman like himself, Murray declared, 'the wilderness provides that perfect relaxation which all jaded minds require.' Other books described adventure in the abstract; Murray told how anyone might go about having one. He became a self-appointed authority on the Adirondacks and everything else connected with the outdoors.

If one could picture oneself in 1869, tired of the city, beset by a threatening financial panic, Murray's words could be moving:

> You choose the locality which best suits your eye and build
> a lodge under unscarred trees, and upon a carpet of moss,
> untrampled by man or beast. There you live in silence, un-
> broken by any sound save such as you yourself may make
> away from all the business and cares of civilized life.

The tales of quiet, untrampled woods, low costs, and available lodges beguiled many a vacationer. Crowds poured into the woods seeking the easy routes, intrepid guides, abundant game, and magnificent vistas 'untouched by man's axe.' What they found was quite different from the Boston minister's description. The stampeding influx of expectant vacationers into the June woods became a bitter and disillusioned people in August. Murray was branded as a colossal (if picturesque) liar.

The response to Murray's book by many a disgruntled 'Fool' is reported with good humor in White's *Adirondack Country* and Cadbury's introduction to the Adirondack Museum's new edition of *Ad-*

ventures in the Wilderness (1970). Some of it came from self-interested sportsmen who were clearly unhappy about giving up their near-monopoly on the vast region. Their dismay at seeing the invading crowds of ordinary tourists, amateur anglers, and even ladies, can easily be imagined. Murray also bore the brunt of opprobrium for the poor transportation, inadequate hotels, and lack of guides. Even the voracious black flies and mosquitoes, of whose appetites Murray had clearly warned, were blamed upon the earnest Boston pastor.

More serious were the questions raised about the region itself and Murray's claims on its behalf. He was accused of murdering invalids, of attracting the wrong sort of people to the Adirondacks, and of creating a situation that severely overtaxed the region's limited facilities. The accusation of 'murder' stemmed from an account in the introduction to the book about a young man, deep in the grip of consumption, who was actually carried into the Adirondacks. After a few

Summer kitchen at Camp Pine Knot, 1880.

months of camp life he was returned to robust health. The story, Murray's critics said, was raising false hopes and perpetrating a 'cruel hoax.' They claimed that invalids coming to the Adirondacks met another fate: the grim reaper.

As it turned out, four years after the publication of Murray's book another young man, this time a physician, was also carried into the Adirondacks. On being helped from the wagon to his hotel bed, the patient heard these words from the guide carrying him: 'Why Doctor, you don't weigh more than a dried lamb-skin.' Doctor — and patient — was Edward Livingston Trudeau, who recovered and went on to achieve international fame for his work at Saranac Lake on tuberculosis therapy.

An Adirondack outing in a Rushton sailing canoe.

Whether or not Murray's book opened the Adirondacks is moot; its effect on the area was enormous. Its effect on the author was greater. Producing a best-seller, reaping a fortune, and becoming a controversial figure surprised Murray, dismayed his congregation, and hastened his departure from his Boston pulpit. His conservative congregation, already chagrined by accusations that their pastor was a liar, was further disturbed by revelations of his hobby — breeding and betting on horses. The church was palpably relieved by his sudden resignation in 1874. Murray's remaining career, reported by Donaldson at length, had little to do with the Adirondacks, although the name 'Adirondack Murray' stuck with him until his death in 1904.

Whether the Adirondacks would have been 'discovered' without Murray's book is debatable, but more than any other man, Murray can be credited with the popularization of the region. Despite the public's outcry, a proliferation of guidebooks, tourist maps, accommodations, and transportation rose to meet the new demand. Murray's book was pivotal. It provided a summary of a lifestyle that was characterized by a golden age of wilderness. It was the precursor of forces that brought the Gilded Age to the Golden Mountains. In the process it helped undo the integrity of the wilderness.

The literary and artistic record of the Adirondacks during this period was impressive. In 1870, *Harper's Monthly* published a piece by Charles Hallock which, although comprising a heavy-handed satire of 'Murray's Rush,' certainly did not inhibit public interest. In this and subsequent years, a host of magazines carried pieces on the Adirondacks, sometimes illustrated by wood-engravings of rural scenes after such artists as Homer Martin, Winslow Homer, Samuel Colman, the Smillie brothers — James D. and George — and by Fred T. Vance and T. S. Jameson. The Adirondack wilderness, 'henceforth to be a grand summer resort for Americans seeking recreation,' as one of the journals put it, soon had some reputable guidebooks as well.

Among the many short-lived guidebooks, those of E. R. Wallace and Seneca Ray Stoddard most effectively captured the spirit — and the market. Wallace's first *Descriptive Guide* appeared in 1872 and was issued in revised editions until 1899. Stoddard, a Glens Falls photographer and artist, initiated his 'Adirondack Illustrated' in 1874. Initially illustrated with his drawings, it later contained his remarkable photographs and continued with annual revisions until two years before the author's death in 1917. Stoddard's photographs (seen throughout this book) are outstanding for their picturesque sensibility, their painterly sensitivity, and their commendable focal clarity. His use of magnesium powder to illuminate evening scenes, with every detail of dress and setting in sharp focus, are as evocative as the paintings of Tait or Homer in revealing the attractions, habits, and customs of the North Woods. In recent years, Stoddard's photographic reputation has finally gained recognition through the admirable publishing efforts of Maitland DeSormo of Saranac Lake, who has issued both Stoddard's diaries and selections of his photographs.

Stoddard's portrayal of the wilderness escape captured the imaginations of young and old alike.

Murray's Rush stirred interest in Albany. In 1872, at the instigation of young Verplanck Colvin, the legislature created a State Park Commission to investigate making a preserve in the Adirondacks. A complete topographical survey was ordered to map the region accurately for the first time. Starting in 1865 on his own and for the next twenty-eight years as a state employee, Colvin hiked the region, climbing and measuring its mountains, mapping its streams and lakes. In time it was his voice that was to call more loudly and more effectively than any other to 'save the Adirondacks.'

Colvin's early reports are filled with a breathless sequence of adventures — descending icy cliffs at midnight, the precious surveying instruments held fast to a rope; being caught on peaks without food. Some years Colvin kept at the job through the winter, working in snowshoes, in fur-lined moccasins, and with toboggans, a far cry from the promises of Murray!

By the early 1880s, with most of the region thoroughly mapped, Colvin's reports became dry records of boundaries and surveys. He summed up how it had changed:

> Viewed from the standpoint of my own exploration, the rapidity with which certain changes take place in the opening up to travel of the wilderness has about it something almost startling. The first romance is gone forever. It is almost as wild and quite as beautiful: but, close behind our exploring footsteps came the blazed line marked with axe upon the trees, the trail soon trodden, the bark shanty, picturesque enough but soon surrounded by a grove of stumps. I find following them the ubiquitous tourist, determined to see all that has been recorded as worth seeing. Where first comes one, the next year there are ten, the year after fully a hundred. Hotels spring up as though by magic and the air resounds with laughter, fun, and jollity. The wild trails, once jammed with logs, are cut clear by the axes of the guides and ladies clamber to the summits of those once untrodden peaks. The genius of change has possession of the land. We cannot control it. When we study the necessities of our people, we would not control it if we could.

Donaldson credits Colvin with the first suggestions for the creation of a state park and with advocating, in a speech as early as 1868, 'the creation of a forest warden and deputies.' In his Second Survey Report (1874) Colvin also urged the wisdom of building an aqueduct from the mountains to New York City, sensing a need that was to inspire the support of downstate conservationists later in the century.

Survey party at Long Lake in 1888.

During his years as superintendent of the state survey, Colvin shared his knowledge of the region in magazine articles and lectures, always presenting it as worth saving for future generations. He was largely responsible for the creation of the Adirondack Forest Preserve in 1885.

In thirty years the Adirondacks had undergone significant change. Two contrasting descriptions of the region illustrate the differences. The first was that of Emmons in 1843: 'It is a region of country as little known and as inadequately explored (except by comparatively few individuals) as the secluded valleys of the Rocky Mountains or the burning plains of Central Africa.'

Just thirty years later a writer in the *New York Times* lamented that the Adirondacks had

> . . . fallen from that estate of fish and solitude for which
> originally celebrated. Railroads, stages, telegraphs and
> hotels have followed in the train of the throng who rushed
> for the wilderness. The desert has blossomed with parasols
> and the waste places are filled with picnic parties, reveling
> in lemonade and sardines. The piano has banished the
> deer from the entire region.

Although somewhat exaggerated, in spirit it was accurate; within thirty years the North Woods had become a booming resort area. The printed word had much to do with it.

CHAPTER 3

THE TREK
TO THE WOODS

Near Ausable in 1892

T HE ARRIVAL of the Gilded Age in the wilderness marked the era of the wilderness tourist, the building of hotels and the creation of the Great Camps. Increases in summer visitors produced demands for improved stagecoach service and expanded inns and guest houses to provide lodging. From the early part of the nineteenth century, before Murray's Rush, resort hotels had existed on the southern and eastern edges of the Adirondacks at such places as North Creek, Keene, Saratoga Springs, Lake Luzerne, and Trenton Falls. They were jumping-off places for the treks into the wilderness by Headley, Hoffman, the intrepid Lady Murray and others. As reports of the beauty of the central Adirondacks reached the outside, the clientele of the early resorts began making trips into the mountains to escape from the boring social routine of the hotels. The solitary male hunter with his guide was being replaced by the family vacation party.

DURING THE LAST third of the nineteenth century the trek to the woods required various combinations of railroad, stagecoach, and steam boat. Although railroads were generally advanced in New York State, they were late in coming to the Adirondacks. But once they approached and penetrated the region, they were the key to the central Adirondacks' development.

The first steam-drawn train in America had barely wobbled the seventeen-mile journey from Albany to Schenectady in 1831 before the railroads were in demand throughout the region. Albany and Saratoga were connected by rail in 1833. By 1845 New York State had 661 miles of railroad. The closest line to the Adirondacks was built in 1850 along the St. Lawrence River valley between Plattsburgh and Ogdensburg.

In 1868 the first line into the Adirondacks reached south from Plattsburgh to Point of Rocks, and by 1874 it was extended to Ausable Forks. In the southeast, Durant's Adirondack Railroad reached North Creek in 1871. By 1875 a railroad had been completed along the entire western side of Lake Champlain. In 1882 a spur line connected Glens Falls on the southeast with Caldwell (Lake George); by 1887 the Chateaugay Railroad reached from Plattsburgh to Saranac Lake (extended to Lake Placid in 1893); and by 1889 railroad lines had reached Tupper Lake from the north and Benson Mines in the west. By 1892 W. Seward Webb's 'Golden Chariot Route,' the Adirondack and St. Lawrence Railroad, traversed the western Adirondacks from Utica to Malone, with spurs reaching Raquette Lake in 1900 and Cranberry Lake from Childwold in 1913. From 1900 until 1930, 1300 feet of track carried the Marion River Carry train back and forth in the heart of the Adirondacks. Change in the guise of technology had come to the area, at first poking into the outer reaches, where railroads connected with

The Way In: Road, Water and Rail

stage lines taking visitors into the central mountains, and finally penetrating well into and through the region.

In these days of excellent roads, automobiles and motels, nothing seems more remote than the era of corduroy dirt roads, buck-board, and stagecoach, but in fact the stagecoach was an important link for about thirty-five years between the central Adirondacks and the outside world, carrying people, parcels, mail, and news. Its coming and going was the event of the day, a ceremony even the busiest would seldom miss. Donaldson extols the drivers as being 'not only kindly and good-natured; they were men of sterling parts, skilled in handling four to six horses, cool and resourceful in danger, hardened to fatigue and exposure.' They certainly had to be tough. Roads were corduroy log, at best narrow and bumpy, full of treacherous holes, thick with sand or deep in mud. The grades were steep, the curves abrupt. A typical day's ride in a Concord coach loaded with passengers and baggage was between thirty and forty miles. Remains of logs that tried the endurance of driver and passenger can occasionally be seen even today on dirt backroads.

Murray described the various routes into the Adirondacks in his usual declamatory style, reciting his preferences and offering his strong recommendations for the quickest and easiest routes. Those

Stagecoach leaving the Prospect House at Blue Mountain Lake for North Creek. The 'Red Line' coach trip of seven hours connected with the railroad for a ten-hour train ride to New York City.

wanting their sport in the southern end of the wilderness could go to Albany, then to Utica and Boonville, and thence by horseback to the Fulton lake chain. Murray noted that 'this entrance was not easy for ladies, nor is the region into which it brings you at all noted for the beauty of its scenery.'

Another route was from the southeast, via Lake George to Warrensburgh, to Minerva, and on to Newcomb and Long Lake. Two other routes started from Whitehall, the terminus of the Saratoga line of the Boston and Albany railroad at the foot of Lake Champlain. Visitors travelling north up the lake by steamboat could make coach connections at Westport or further up the lake at Port Kent. What Murray called the 'mere tourist route' led to Elizabethtown and on to Keene, at the very eastern edge of the high peaks.

But the preferred route, which Murray recommended as the 'easy and quick route,' passed 'through some of the sublimest scenery in the world.' In his own words:

> I leave Boston Monday morning, we will say at eight o'clock, on the Boston and Albany Railroad. At East Albany we connect with the Troy train; at Troy, with the Saratoga train, which lands you at Whitehall, Lake Champlain, at nine o'clock p.m. Going on board, you sit down to a dinner, abundant in quantity and well served; after which you retire to your stateroom, or, if so inclined, roll an arm-chair to the hurricane deck and enjoy that rarest of treats, a steamboat excursion on an inland lake by moonlight. At 4:30 a.m. you are opposite Burlington, Vermont, and by the time you are dressed the boat slides alongside the dock at Port Kent, on the New York side of the lake. You enter a coach which stands waiting, and, after a ride of six miles in the cool morning air, you alight at the Ausable House, Keeseville. Here, you array yourself for the woods, and eating a hearty breakfast, you seat yourself in the coach at 7 a.m., the whip cracks, the horses spring, and you are off on a fifty-six mile ride over a plank road, which brings you, at 5 p.m., to Martin's on the lower Saranac, where your guide, with his narrow shell drawn up upon the beach, stands waiting you. This is the shortest, easiest, and beyond all odds the best route to the Adirondacks. You leave Boston or New York Monday at 8 a.m., and reach your guide Tuesday at 5 p.m.

Murray's 'indispensable guide' was an important ingredient in the increase in the number of travelers. The guides, as one writer of the period said, were 'steady, intelligent, and experienced men, [who] can be hired at all the taverns [and] who will provide books, tents, and

Guides waiting at Raquette Lake.

everything required for a trip.' Each guide provided a guideboat, a unique, lightweight, double-ended rowboat designed to be carried on the guide's shoulders. With this durable little craft, twelve to sixteen feet in length, portages from lake to lake or from stream to stream were easily accomplished. Early models of these perfect unions of form and function are valuable collector's items today and new ones are still being handcrafted along the same lines.

These same entry routes were described by Wallace and Stoddard in their guidebooks, which were modified as roads improved. In 1871 the extension of the Adirondack Railroad from Saratoga to North Creek opened an approach from the south to the Raquette Lake region. Other lines soon followed. Regular stagecoach service was initiated on previously lightly used routes in the 1870s, and by 1878 steamboats were plying several Adirondack lakes. What a rare sight it must have been on July 4, 1878, to see John Philip Sousa's band playing on the main deck of the steamer *Water Lily* on lower Saranac Lake! Other steamboat lines developed about the same time on Raquette Lake and Blue Mountain, and were subsequently expanded by William West Durant, the son of the Adirondack Railroad builder, Thomas C. Durant. In 1882, Wallace's *Guide* noted that 'Between Blue Mountain Lake, by Tupper and the Saranac Lake, there is now a continuous line of steamers, affording close connections with each other, via Raquette, Forked and Long Lakes and the Raquette River.' Durant's fleet, named *Killoquah, Utowana, Irocosia,* and *Toowarlandah,* plied the lakes into the early 1920s, long after stagecoach and buckboard had been replaced by the railroad.

Dreams of a region rich in iron and timber, only lacking modern transportation to get it out, inspired many a railroad scheme that produced worthless stock and nothing more. From 1830 on, countless plans were drawn, surveys prepared, and stock issued for companies that never materialized. In the 1840s and 50s, hundreds of thousands of acres were acquired and lines were planned to enter from north and south and to cross the Adirondacks from east to west, all to gain access to the riches above and below ground. Little attention was given to the effects of the railroads on the forests. The schemes that did finally mature brought with them what Hochschild calls 'a new era for the Central Adirondacks.'

Two names figure prominently in this era: Thomas C. Durant, who planned to extend the Adirondack Railroad from North Creek north to the St. Lawrence and open up the Raquette Lake and Blue Mountain Lake area; and William Seward Webb, who built the Adirondack and St. Lawrence railroad in 1892, connecting Herkimer to Malone farther to the north.

The Killoquah, No. 1, *first launched in 1879.*

Railroad Builders

IF THE Reverend Murray's book can be regarded as the leading psychological factor that opened the Adirondack wilderness, it was the railroad builders who provided the physical vehicle. Taking on the challenge of assembling rights-of-way, raising capital, clearing road, and laying track required men of strong will and determination. Two such men were Thomas C. Durant and William Seward Webb.

The network of railroads that tied the nation together during the 1860s inspired investors to seek other opportunities to build new lines and share in the rapid appreciation of lands contiguous to the tracks. Skills learned out West were applied to the Adirondack forests and mountains. Lumber and iron could be brought out and tourists brought in: that was the scheme of the Adirondack Railroad, a line originally planned in the 1850s but bankrupt by 1863 when it passed into the control of Thomas C. Durant.

Durant was a graduate surgeon who abandoned an Albany medical practice to become an exporter of flour and grain. But it was railroads that fascinated him and he was instrumental in building several lines

Thomas C. Durant.
From Harper's Weekly,
1870.

through the Midwest. During these activities he had the idea of building a transcontinental line. From 1861 till the driving of the last spike eight years later, he was vice president, general manager, and acting president of the Union Pacific.

In 1863 Durant saw challenge and opportunity in the bankrupt Adirondack Railroad and reorganized it under a special legislative act (April 27, 1863) as 'the Adirondack Company.' The new charter was very broad, conferring the privileges of a land, railroad, mining and manufacturing company to the new organization. The line was planned to run from Saratoga through the heart of the mountains to Ogdensburg. Later the company was given the option of either Lake Ontario or the St. Lawrence as a terminus. Durant's enterprise was supported in 1864 by an editorial in the *New York Times:*

> The Adirondack Company, improving one of the privileges of their charter, and in order to develop the wealth of their enormous possessions in that region, are building a railroad, the first object of which is to reach their mines and forests, and the ultimate one to strike the St. Lawrence with its branches at different points, so as to draw into its channel the bulk of the travel and transportation between our seaboard and Central Canada. The fact that this work is prosecuted under the direct supervision of Thomas C. Durant, Esq., one of the principal stockholders of the Company, and one of the ablest railway men of the country, is a sufficient guarantee for its rapid progress; and with its completion, the Adirondack region will become a suburb of New York.

The *Dictionary of American Biography* describes Durant: 'reticent and quiet in manner, [and one] able to excite his subordinates to extraordinary exertion. In his associates he aroused deep antagonism or warm admiration.' Durant remained untainted by the Credit Mobilier scandal surrounding the Union Pacific.

The franchise of the railroad required that the initial stretch should extend north from Saratoga sixty miles. In 1865 twenty-five miles were opened; after a four-year hiatus, twelve more miles of track were laid, followed by twelve miles in 1870 and eleven miles in 1871. By 1871 the line attained the requisite distance by reaching North Creek. There it stopped. Funds were exhausted and the panic of 1873 ended all work. The line remained dormant until 1943 when it was extended to the McIntyre mines at Tahawus.

For a brief moment in 1901, fleeting fame struck the North Creek Station. Dashing down from Mount Marcy to reach Buffalo and the side of dying President McKinley, Theodore Roosevelt raced for a waiting train. He reached the North Creek station at 4:39 A.M. on September 14, there to be informed that he was the president of the United States.

At first glance, the short line Durant completed might appear a negligible influence on the opening of the Adirondacks. But the line did transport thousands of tourists from Saratoga and was an important gateway to the region. In fact, it carried over 120,000 passengers in its first five years of operation. Overshadowing the modest trackage was the assembled land of the Adirondack Company, estimated at 700,000 acres throughout the central Adirondacks, in Essex, Herkimer, Franklin, St. Lawrence, and Hamilton counties.

Not nearly as well supported editorially as Durant's venture was the building of the Adirondack and St. Lawrence Railroad, the only line running through the mountains. When William Seward Webb set out in 1890 to connect Herkimer to the main line of the New York Central and then run track to Malone and on toward Montreal, the scheme was attacked by the *New York Times.* In a June 7, 1891 editorial the *Times,* outraged by this breach of the wilderness, reversed its position of less than thirty years before. It was considerably more suspicious and had this to say of the railroad, its builder, and his kind.

> It will be safer and better for the State to waste no time in getting promises from Dr. W. Seward Webb or his representatives. The builders of railroads are notoriously among the most aggressive and enterprising of created beings. With them possession is nine points of the law, and they trust to the delays and uncertainties of the law itself for the other point.

There are curious parallels between the origins and careers of Durant and Webb. Both were scions of prominent Revolutionary families; like Durant, Webb became a physician, forsook medicine for finance, and finally turned to railroad building. After marrying Lila Vanderbilt in 1881, Webb was persuaded to abandon medicine and turn his energies and intellect to Wall Street. After successfully leading the Wagner Palace Car Company, he set his sights on building a railroad through the Adirondacks. In 1890 Webb obtained the incorporation of the St. Lawrence and Adirondack Railway. The well-capitalized plan for the enterprise included the purchase of 143,494 acres in northern Hamilton and Herkimer counties.

In the face of editorial opposition, construction pushed forward in 1891 and 1892. Through monumental effort and extraordinary organization, the job was completed in only eighteen months, despite a desperate shortage of power machinery for clearing land, grading, laying track, and building roads. Once in operation, Webb leased and finally sold the railroad to the New York Central. Finding it difficult to maintain control over the original 225 square miles of holdings, Webb sold off 75,000 acres to the state and, a few years later, all but 40,000 of the remainder. He still retained certain rights of access, including the installation of a telegraph operating from his private preserve, Nehasane, to his home in Shelburne, Vermont, and three private railroad stations. The public was barred from his stations and trains were permitted to stop only when a guest could produce a special pass issued by Dr. W. Seward Webb.

In *Conquering the Wilderness,* Charles H. Burnett's history of the Adirondack and St. Lawrence Railroad, Webb is described as popular with his employees. 'By his executive ability and talent for organization, he turned a decadent enterprise into a highly successful one, second to none.' Like Durant, Webb was accustomed to attempt the impossible and attain it by force of personality and will.

By opening new areas to vacationers, Durant and Webb had performed a great public service. Tourists, individuals seeking private campsites, hunting and fishing clubs, hotel builders, and lumbermen now had easy access to the central Adirondacks. By 1895, the end of the golden years of the Adirondacks, lakes that had been two days' travel from the nearest railroad were now within sight of the new line. Remote forest retreats blossomed into thriving summer resorts. Before the railroads, much of the Adirondacks was inaccessible except to those who could afford to penetrate the forest by coach, by guideboat, or on foot. The railroads, in improving access to the mountains and lakes, did not leave the woods unscarred, and thus inadvertently helped foster public concern for what wilderness remained.

Dr. W. Seward Webb.

THE TREK to the woods by vacationers stimulated the enterprising settler to open his doors to travelers. Stagecoach inns deep in the woods became 'hotels' to accommodate the hardy adventurer to the wilderness. William Chapman White quotes one observer who, looking around the woods shortly after 1870, commented: 'The day is coming when it's all going to be one vast boardinghouse. You can still go to dinner in a flannel shirt but as the snobby New Yorker and snobbier wife turn up, the old set fades away.' It never really got quite that bad, but hotels and boarding houses continued to spring up all over.

White sums up much about Adirondack hotels in the history of the Forge House, a small but popular hotel near the First Lake of the Fulton Chain.

Hotels and Hotelkeepers

> Opened in 1871, it was managed first by a young couple who had trekked into the wilderness a few years earlier carrying their baby son in a pack basket. The hotel began as a building of rough-sawn spruce boards, with thirteen rooms and attic space for guides. Its dining room had two dining tables, one for guests, one for guides. Year by year thereafter it grew larger and fancier. Like many of the hotels, it frequently changed hands, although no hotel changed quite as often; before the Forge House burned in 1924 it had had twenty-one different proprietors.

Murray, in his chapter on hotels, mentions five that had been established in the early 1850s and 60s: Bartlett's, Mother Johnson's at Raquette Falls, Uncle Palmer's, Martin's, and Paul Smith's, whose eponymous proprietors were convivial and vivid characters.

In 1854 Bill Martin was the first to build a hotel in the central Adirondacks with the sole purpose of attracting people of leisure and wealth. His hotel on Lower Saranac Lake was extolled by Wallace in his first guidebook as 'one of the far-famed gateways to the wilderness, a most desirable tarrying place for all in quest of health or sporting recreation.' Martin and other early hotelkeepers furnished travelers with Murray's complete list of camping necessities, including tents, provisions, and guides. In spite of — or perhaps because of — this, the camping tradition led the wealthy to conclude that owning their own campsites would be a more comfortable arrangement and they set about first leasing and then purchasing land. Eventually they built the tent platforms and simple cabins that preceded the Great Camps.

The Forge House at Old Forge, from the railroad station.

The location of the early hotels on Raquette, Saranac, and St. Regis lakes was instrumental in developing interest in these regions. Bartlett's, in a beautiful, remote setting on Upper Saranac Lake, was run by a genial host who had come to the area as early as had Martin. As with several other hotels with great reputations it was the owner's wife's fine cooking, congenial manner, and managerial skills that made

*Early guest lodging:
An Adirondack lean-to
at Pine Knot; a bark
teepee at Nehasane.*

*Prospect House, Blue
Mountain Lake. Sur-
rounding the windmill
is the white deer corral.*

for a successful venture, often offsetting the occasionally cantan-
kerous nature of the male host. At one hotel, a wealthy man who had
arrived with a large party of guests, was annoyed to find the dining
room filled. He stated loudly and nastily that he was unaccustomed to
waiting. When his party was shown to their table it was obviously the
best in the room, set with the whitest linen, fresh flowers. When asked
the cost, the owner refused payment. 'But I can't accept that,' said the
guest. 'Why, I couldn't possibly return here again if I don't pay you
now.' 'That's just what I thought, mister,' replied the owner. 'Good-
bye, sir.'

Successful resort centers grew in only a few places: on the shores of
Lake George, Lake Placid, and Schroon Lake, where rows of hotels
stood side by side. Outside of the established colonies, hotels were isolated, each on its own lake. A backwoods hotel's success depended
upon transportation; for most that meant four- and six-horse stage-
coaches. Stages continued to run for some years after the railroads
came in, but many a remote hotel failed when the railroad passed it by.
Backwoods places like Paul Smith's, deep in the woods, had rustic
charm. To compete, the lakefront hotels provided sheer luxury.

One of the most extraordinary hotels ever built anywhere was the
Prospect House, overlooking Blue Mountain Lake. Hochschild de-
votes an entire chapter to this 'epochal project' started in 1879. Stimu-

Above, *Prospect House
at Blue Mountain
Lake.* Left, *porch of
Prospect House, around
1882, with Durant family
group at right.*

Right, *Apollos (Paul)
Smith at age 53 (a
Seneca Ray Stoddard
photograph taken on
September 22, 1878).*
Above, *Paul Smith's
Hotel, St. Regis
Lake, 1873.*

lated by the influx of tourists to the area, Frederick C. Durant left his father's sugar-refining business in New York City to build the hotel. His uncle, Thomas C. Durant, had shifted his interest from the North Creek railroad venture to developing the region for tourism and, along with his son William West Durant, began projects just to the west, in the Raquette Lake area.

What Cousin Frederick built was a large wooden box of a building, T-shaped, with a 225-foot-long façade facing the lake. Six stories high, it was built from lumber cut on the spot in his sawmill and put together by local craftsmen. It had twenty-foot-wide piazzas on three sides, high ceilings, and generally resembled the architecture of The Grand Hotel and United States Hotel in Saratoga Springs. Wallace's 1882 *Guide* said: 'No structure of equal magnitude or magnificence has elsewhere been attempted.'

Of the Prospect House, Donaldson writes:

> At the time it was the largest and by far the most luxurious hotel in the woods, and its erection on that remote spot, thirty miles from a railway, was a stupendous and remarkable achievement. Structurally it had no beauty and was merely a gaunt, ungainly pile of piazzas and windows, but inwardly it contained the latest refinements in comfort and convenience.

The Prospect House had three hundred rooms, running water in every room, a primitive sort of steam heat to ward off the autumn chill, and a two-story outhouse reached from the second floor piazza so guests on the upper floors would not have the inconvenience of descending to ground level. More astonishingly, every bedroom in this remote hotel had an electric light powered by two Edison dynamos run on steam from a wood fire.

A few Adirondack hotels maintained their reputations and enjoyed fabulous prosperity for many years. Without question, the most famous was Paul Smith's. Stories about its founder form the stuff of Adirondack legends. Known as Paul by everyone, the giant Vermonter who built the sprawling complex on Lower St. Regis Lake was born Appolos Smith. His success was built on his wife's ability to cook good dinners and his own skill at telling good stories. With exceptional shrewdness and foresight he built the most remarkable establishment ever seen in the mountains.

Smith is described by Donaldson as a 'respector of no persons,' and he gradually became a fad. Paying little heed to social or economic standing, Smith could (and did) reject or accept any guest for his own good reasons. He had a sense of humor that had a Yankee edge, and in time acquired a reputation that was an attraction equal to anything in

*Paul Smith —
A Legend*

the Adirondacks. He had an infallible charm, an ability to make close friends with the wealthy and important. One of the latter said: 'He was one-third court jester, one-third shrewd beyond measure, and one-third robber baron who robbed the rich to care for the rich — himself."

Born in 1825, he lived eighty-seven years, spanning the Adirondack's opening, development, and flowering. When he could get away from working on a canal boat between Lake Champlain and the Hudson River, Smith came to the Adirondacks regularly as a young man to hunt and fish. He became a habitué at Loon Lake, where other guests sought him out as a guide and hunting companion. They encouraged him to establish his own inn. He did, and in 1852 Smith's first venture opened near Loon Lake. Accommodations were primitive — a large living room, kitchen, dormitory overhead, and a bar on the premises. No provisions were made for ladies. Board and lodging was $1.25 per day; a guide's service for the day was $2.00.

The strictly male retreat caught on. A select patronage of wealthy lawyers, doctors, and businessmen enjoyed Smith's inimitable humor and hospitality, and passed the word along to friends. In fact they enjoyed life at Smith's so much that they asked the couple to improve and expand their accommodations, offering to finance them. Smith found a choice spot on Lower St. Regis Lake, ten miles northeast of Saranac Lake, and in 1858 purchased fifty acres of land. The original building of seventeen bedrooms was completed and opened for the summer of 1859, soon becoming one of the best known and most amazingly successful summer resorts in the Adirondacks.

'Paul Smith's' was raised on a sign over the entrance and to its end bore no other name. The first building and its many additions eventually grew from a backwoods hotel to a sprawling complex with 500 rooms. From the beginning, Smith shrewdly reinvested into building expansion and land acquisition, buying larger and larger blocks of land until his holdings were between 30,000 and 40,000 acres. He realized very early that the real industry of the region would be the summer tourists. Wealthy guests who asked to lease land for campsites came back to Smith to negotiate purchases. He continued to sell campsites to the prominent families of the country; his hotel was the social center and provided supplies for the permanent summer colony. Paul Smith's became a 'caravansary for wealth and its satellites.' Donaldson describes the building in its heyday as having 'no great beauty inside or out, not even of location; but it held some indescribable charm for great numbers of people — a charm which, in the last analysis, traced back to the owner's personality.'

Typical of his many quips is one retold by William Chapman White. Hearing that one of his coaches to the railroad had been held up and robbed on the way out, he laughed: 'Fool of a highwayman, holding up passengers after they've left here. What did he expect to find on them?' Many guests noticed his shrewdness. He was once told by a clerk, 'I forgot to put a charge for a pair of rubber boots on the bill of some guest, and I've forgotten which one.' Smith said, 'Put a charge of a pair of boots on every guest's bill. Most of 'em won't notice it.'

By the time Paul Smith died in 1912, automobiles were regulars in the Adirondacks. In his last days he rode in one, not realizing that it would change the course of Adirondack life. After his death, the hotel continued under the direction of his two sons. As the 1930 season came to a close the hotel burned to the ground and was never rebuilt. After the death of the sons, the entire estate was converted into a college, with special courses in hotel management and forest conservation. It was named simply Paul Smith's College.

With Smith's death a curtain fell on an era. His lifetime had spanned the long transition from the oxen to automobile, from corduroy road to railroad to highway, from rough outdoor living to the luxury of the Great Camps.

Upper Saranac Lake

Clubs and Preserves

THE ROAD to the woods that led men to the resort hotels also induced them to acquire their own land for hunting and fishing. Some were ambitious enough to build campsites for their families; others were content to form clubs and share in the ownership or lease of vast tracts of land. Hotels overshadowed the private camps on certain lakes, such as Blue Mountain Lake, while the same conditions fostered the development of camps on other lakes, such as the St. Regis area. But in the forest areas away from the hotels and stagecoach roads, vast areas could be acquired from the state at bargain prices.

Three types of land ownership emerged during the 1870s and 80s: the campsite located on a lakeshore or mountainside; the club consisting of joint membership, sometimes with a central lodge and outlying individual campsites; and the private preserve of thousands of acres containing a luxurious Adirondack hunting lodge.

Purchase of large land holdings exclusively for hunting and fishing occurred as early as 1848, when Benjamin Brandreth established Brandreth Park on 26,000 acres. This later became the Brandreth Preserve and is still owned by his descendants. In 1875, an act was passed requiring an association of private individuals to acquire a charter, permitting private preserves on state lands. This had the effect of encouraging large land assemblages; that is, until all state-owned lands in the Adirondacks were withdrawn from sale in 1883. By then, state ownership consisted of fragmented parcels in and around the great private holdings and totaled about 700,000 acres.

By the 1890s more than sixty associations owned thousands of acres, to which should be added the thousands of acres in the hands of large-camp owners. In 1893, the State Forest Commission reported

The Hooker family tent platforms at Upper St. Regis Lake.

that 'fully one-fourth of the Great Forest of Northern New York is held in private preserves by clubs, associations, or individuals, used for fishing and hunting, for summer resorts, or . . . sale of timber.' Vast acreage was closed to public access, the clubs setting out patrolled boundaries, protected by caretakers and guides.

Several private clubs owned or leased holdings of over 100,000 acres. Among the earliest was the Adirondack Club, formed in 1877 as a private fish and game club. Later renamed the Tahawus Club, the organization leased its 96,000 acres of land from the Adirondack Iron and Steel Company. Buildings on the abandoned mining site were used as clubhouses and guest cottages.

The first association to acquire its own lands was organized in 1878 as the Bisby Club. In 1890 the Adirondack League Club was formed and both clubs merged in 1893. By 1894, club acreage included 116,000 acres and its leases controlled the exclusive fishing and hunting privileges on a contiguous parcel of 75,000 acres. The total preserve amounted to nearly 200,000 acres, or over 275 square miles, containing 93,000 acres of virgin forest and more than twenty-five lakes, streams, and ponds. An ongoing policy of forest management has offset taxes, providing the owners of the shares with regular income, and their shares have increased in value.

For its certificate of incorporation the club stated its object: 'to acquire a tract of land in the Adirondack region, and to maintain the same as a fishing and hunting preserve, and as a pleasure resort for its members.' The first report of the club's trustees in 1891 represents the aims and spirit of the many preserves and associations that were then being formed:

> Four distinct motives may be said to have contributed to its organization, and its membership is made up of gentlemen who share those motives in varying proportions. These have been, First, the public spirit of the philanthropist who wished to protect from spoliation the richest timber tract in the Adirondacks, and conserve the water supply to the rivers and canals of the State; Second, the ardor of the sportsman, who desired to secure and perpetuate the splendid hunting and fishing upon this tract, and to establish a vast preserve for the propagation of every kind of game; Third, the eagerness of the lover of the forest, the lake and the mountains, to seek health and relaxation in Nature's greatest sanitarium; and Fourth, the zeal of the investor looking for the best investment of his money.

To the northeast, in the area of the high peaks near Keene, the Adirondack Mountain Reserve was formed in 1887 'to preserve the

Ausable Lakes, rivers, and adjacent forests in their natural beauty, and to prevent them from being injured; to restock the waters with fish and to protect the game. Places of interest are to be rendered more accessible by roads and trails.' Later renamed the Ausable Lake and Mountain Club and ultimately simply the Ausable Club, the 28,000 acres owned by the organization contain some of the most scenic areas of the Adirondacks.

Associations, such as the Tahawus Club, the Adirondack League Club, and the Ausable Club, maintained central clubhouses for members and leased campsites for private cabins. The structures varied in design from the simple to the elaborate: the main building at Tahawus was a simple frame building used originally by the mining company as a boarding house; the Adirondack League Club had three large main buildings; and the Ausable Club an elaborate hotel-like building. Central dining rooms, recreation rooms, and accommodations were straightforward examples of simple, mountain resorts. Outlying cabins were rustic, reflecting the owners' tastes, and were built by locally available craftsmen. The Adirondack League Club has many fine examples of rustic camps created by professional architects; one of the club members, Augustus D. Shepard, was responsible for several of the buildings, many of which are described in his book *Camps in the Woods* (1931). Another club member was the famous architect Stan-

The Ausable Club main lodge.

ford White, although it is unrecorded whether he did any more than enjoy the club's hunting and fishing. In contrast to the more finished camps elsewhere, the rough camps of the Ausable Club, deep in the high-peak country, remain untouched examples characteristic of the camps of the last century.

By 1893 total private and association land holdings were 941,036 acres, and a list of the owners and members read like a who's who of Eastern society and state politics. It was during this era that many of the important Great Camps were started by Durant at Sagamore and Uncas, Garvan at Kill Kare, Vanderbilt at Kildare Club, Pruyn at Santanoni, Litchfield at Litchfield Park, and Webb at Nehasane.

Motives for assembling large tracts ostensibly for hunting and fishing were mixed with less benign intentions — railroad building, logging, or just plain land speculation. William Seward Webb, for example, acquired almost 200,000 acres as part of his plan to build the Adirondack Railroad. Others, like Ferris J. Meigs and Robert C. Pruyn, acquired holdings for logging purposes. They and others eventually built some of the most splendid of the Great Camps.

The early camp owners were leaders in the conservation movement in New York State, and to a certain extent, in the country, their pressure exerting a special influence upon the crucial state legislation. Ironically, it is the preservation of those Great Camps whose owners worked hardest for these ideals that is now in jeopardy.

Colonel Loring's Ausable Club.

CHAPTER 4

THE CAMP ERA BEGINS

A family portrait at Brandreth Lake.

AT THE END of the Civil War a new era dawned for the nation and the Adirondacks. Aptly dubbed *The Gilded Age* in Mark Twain and Charles Dudley Warner's novel by that name, it was characterized in the Adirondacks by the region's increasing attractiveness to high society.

By the mid-nineteenth century, Saratoga, on the southern edge of the Adirondacks, had become a socially desirable resort. Called 'Queen of the Spas,' Saratoga was every bit as fashionable as other watering-holes of American society, including Newport, Narragansett, and Cape May. August was the high point of the season, attracting the elite for the month's races of the Saratoga Association for the Improvement of the Breed of Horses. Society flocked from as far off as Chicago to promenade on the porches of the great hotels, drink and bathe in the local spas, and exchange gossip.

Soon, trouble began to brew. The resort's main attraction, its 'curative' waters, was so heavily exploited that the springs began to go dry. At the same time, Saratoga went through a Newport-like transition. Newer and more ostentatious money came in; this element was mixed with a sporting crowd, attracted by the races and gambling casinos. Saratoga was becoming vulgar, and the older members of Society reacted as they commonly did when the blemish of the *nouveaux arrivés* tainted the tranquillity and congeniality of established money; they retreated to the large and isolated hotels along the northern lakes — Lake George, the Saranacs, and Blue Mountain.

The central Adirondacks' spreading reputation and the new luxuries they sported provided an alternative to the gaucheries of Saratoga. By the 1870s and early 1880s, the emergence of suitable inns and the availability of local trout and venison combined with the magnificent settings to make the region fashionable. One New York society editor wrote in 1883:

> The grand masquerade ball at the Prospect House was one of the greatest events of the Season. The large and magnificent parlor was brilliantly illuminated with a thousand electric lights and filled to repletion with the elite of every clime. Such an amount of dazzling beauty, such beautiful figures robed in costly attire, such a brilliant flow of wit and humor seldom grace the halls of prince or potentate.

The requisite social cachet had not before been bestowed on the Adirondacks, as it had been to New England or the Jersey Shore, but now, in the curious and fickle way Society adopts a fashion or a place, the Adirondacks were deemed desirable. It became popular to spend July at the seashore and August in the mountains. One of the reasons for this choice had to do with Adirondack weather. The ladies, not

The Social Life

55

wishing to return to town with skin darkened by sun and spray, elected to retire to the Adirondacks toward the season's end to regain their lily-white complexions. The pesky black fly provided reason enough for staying away from the North Woods in July.

Magazines such as *Frank Leslie's Illustrated* and *Harper's Weekly* frequently showed the natural beauty of the region, the camps of the wealthy, and the lifestyles of the rich. Social columns reported their comings and goings, and as more and more recognizable 'names' of the Gilded Age migrated north, the Adirondacks were adopted as both *du monde* and *de rigueur*.

The height of the season in places like Paul Smith's or the Prospect House was as fashionable as any of the seashore retreats of society.

An 'Idem' on Upper St. Regis Lake.

The color, characters, and the countryside of a day at Paul Smith's were described by Charles Hallock in the pages of *Field and Stream:*

> Great is the stir of the long summer evenings — ribbons fluttering on the piazzas, silks rustling in the dress promenade; ladies in short mountain suits, fresh from an afternoon picnic; embryo sportsmen in velveteen and corduroys of approved cut, descanting learnedly of backwoods experience; excursion parties returning, laden with trophies of trout and pond lilies; stages arriving top heavy with trunks, rifle cases, and hampers; guides intermingling, proffering services, or arranging trips for the morrow; pistols shooting at random; invalids bundled in blankets, propped up in chairs; old gents distracted, vainly perusing their papers; fond lovers strolling; dowagers scheming; mosquitoes devouring; the supper-bell ringing. Anon some millionaire Nimrod or piscator of marked renown drags in from a weary day with a basket of unusual weight, or perchance a fawn cut down before its time. He receives his honors with that becoming dignity which reticence impresses, and magnificently tips a twenty-dollar note to his trusty guide. After supper there is a generous flow of champagne to a selected few upon the western piazza, and the exploits of the day are recounted and compared. The parlors grow noisy with music and dancing; silence and smoke prevail in the cardroom.

The opportunities provided by land speculation, timber profiteering, and railroad building spread among the board rooms of the rich and powerful, passing on to drawing-room conversation. Hunting and fishing parties combined 'roughing it' for a couple of weeks with inquiries into North Woods land opportunities. Soon the male-only Adirondack world was graced by wives who could find social pleasures in the luxury hotels. The Adirondacks began to attract its own band of supporters, regulars who would return each year.

For some vacationers the Adirondacks' main attraction was the congenial social atmosphere and activities of the hotels. An editorial in an 1891 issue of *Garden and Forest* supports this attitude: 'To many of them, woods and mountains offer few attractions in themselves. . . . It is the crowd and excitement which is expected to restore wasted energy. The recuperating force of personal contact with nature is not thought of.'

But some were drawn to the Adirondacks for the privacy and solitude found in wilderness settings — miraculously within a day's journey from Wall Street. William Dix, the editor of *Town and Country,*

Lean-to at Under the Hemlocks, Raquette Lake.

described 'Summer Life in Luxurious Adirondack Camps' in 1903, commenting:

> Few who have not lived this healthful, invigorating life can appreciate its wonderful charm. It is a return to nature after ten months of wearying city life with ceaseless formalities and responsibilities. Here the busy professional man or financier can find real rest and surcease from business as in no other way, and it is an interesting phase of American social life and decidedly significant. . . . As society has grown more and more complex, the swing of the pendulum goes more and more toward simplicity for the vacation.

Wallace's and Stoddard's guidebooks mentioned the names of prominent families who had established campsites surrounding the hotels. Such acceptability combined with the adventurous atmosphere was inducement enough to impel even the most passive industrialists to either secure their own campsites or form rustic mountain clubs. Private railroad cars were assembled in New York and headed north with family, servants, baggage, and provisions for the August stay. Choices of site varied with personal tastes and familiarity with mountain and lake, ease of access, or personal associations.

In her reminiscences in *Camp Chronicles,* Mildred Phelps Stokes Hooker, daughter of a New York financier, recalls that her father brought his family to Paul Smith's and went into rough camp on a nearby island. The family slept under canvas tents on balsam branches and bathed in the lake. Soon the Stokeses and other families purchased sites on the St. Regis lakes, Saranac Lake, and Raquette Lake. 'Roughing it' was part of the attraction; luxury came later.

Having established permanent campsites, tent platforms were built for reuse each year. Preparations and the journey north for the summer of 1883 were recalled by Mrs. Hooker:

> Busy packing all the morning, Patrick left in the afternoon with horses, Muggins and Sport (a pug and a setter), and a truckload of freight. Papa chartered what they call a special parlor horse car direct from 42nd Street to Ausable for $100, and we take in it our horses, carriage, all camping outfits, extra trunks, stores, etc. They go to Plattsburg and arrive tomorrow evening. Then to Ausable where the freight will be taken off by wagons to Paul Smith's. . . . Baggage, etc., for summer campaign of the Stokes family [included:]
>
> Anson Phelps Stokes, wife, seven children, one niece (Mabel Slade), about ten servants, Miss Rondell, one coachman, three horses, two dogs, one carriage, five large boxes of tents, three cases of wine, two packages of stovepipe, two stoves, one bale china, one iron pot, four washstands, one barrel of hardware, four bundles of poles, seventeen cots and seventeen mattresses, four canvas packages, one buckboard, five barrels, one-half barrel, two tubs of butter, one bag coffee, one chest tea, one crate china, twelve rugs, four milkcans, two drawing boards, twenty-five trunks, thirteen small boxes, one boat, one hamper.

The social life of families like the Stokeses revolved around visiting neighbors for 'teas,' entertaining guests, and enjoying the outdoors. Pretense was little tolerated and Mrs. Hooker recalls that 'dressing' was informal. 'I do like the freedom of this place in the way of dress,' she quotes her mother. 'Even calls are made in flannel suits and gentlemen wear knickerbockers and coarse stockings.' Mrs. Hooker does, however, recall seeing 'one of our neighbors in full evening dress and bedecked with diamonds paddling in a canoe with a man in a "boiled" shirt en route to a dinner at the Vanderbilts!' And although notions of the rustic life prevailed, the Stokeses imported a White House chef in 1884 to 'help' in the kitchen.

As the St. Regis lakes became dotted with campsites, the competitiveness of Wall Street titans was transfered to sailing on the quiet waters of Adirondack lakes. Regular weekend regattas were held and the simple trophies were treasured as though they were engraved silver bowls.

A house full of guests was common. The Garvans at Kamp Kill Kare regularly invited the entire Yale and Harvard baseball teams to the camp. Block *Y*'s and *H*'s would square off against each other in August away from Cambridge and New Haven for the entertainment of family and friends under the pines. The previous owner of the camp,

Kamp Kill Kare:
'Venice' on Lake Kora.

Lieutenant Governor Timothy Woodruff, kept a trained bear. He also imported a gondola from Venice in 1898 to round out his fleet of boats, barges, and canoes.

Hunting lodges like Alfred G. Vanderbilt's Sagamore, with sleeping space for up to one hundred guests, offered that peculiar graciousness of the English country seat, where guests might see their host occasionally at the dining table while enjoying the full hospitality of the estate. For the camp-bound traveler who didn't care for the hunting, fishing, hiking, or boating, indoor bowling alleys, amusement halls, and putting greens were available. Some lodge owners thrived in their role as genial hosts, raconteurs, and companions, but others simply enjoyed sharing their table.

In her 1922 edition of *Etiquette*, Emily Post devoted a chapter to manners for the house party in the Adirondacks. Palatial displays in the Newport style were rejected for the somewhat more subtle satisfactions derived from less conspicuous consumption. Rustic charm was emphasized as an essential ingredient; this simple life of creature discomfort was to be *enjoyed*. Part of a host's duty, however, was assuring his guests that although removed from city conveniences, they would not find 'roughing it' a hardship. Although the thought of being away from one's maid or valet might initially discourage a guest, Post was quick to point out that the primitive appearance was only superficial.

> Let no one, however, think that this is a 'simple' (by that meaning either easy or inexpensive) form of entertainment! Imagine the budget! A dozen guides, teams and drivers, natives to wash and clean and help the cook; food for two or three dozen people sent hundreds of miles by express!

Stories filled the pages of *Broadway Magazine, Town and Country,* and *Field and Stream* of merry weekends under 'an infinitude of azure,' where the house guest could 'pass through leafy green tunnels' and 'paddle out into breeze-rippled surfaces.' This scene was repainted in countless ways to countless readers in the 1890s and early 1900s:

A Romantic Setting

> Suddenly from around a wooded point, a tiny fleet of canoes dart out into the glittering water containing rosy-faced, white-clad girls and athletic looking young men in summer flannels. Some of the girls are paddling. Their sleeves are rolled up to the elbow and their hair shines, uncovered in the sun. You hear the tinkle of a mandolin, a snatch of song and little ripples of laughter, and the lake seems all at once to be smiling and human.

This was the setting Theodore Dreiser used for *An American Tragedy,* with Big Moose Lake as the background for Chester Gillette's story. Dreiser's 'fiction' actually occurred, and its passages on the social life and activities are among the more accurate descriptions of the era.

Even though early hunting and fishing trips provided male excuses to leave the constraints of domestic life, women were frequent companions in the woods. Clubs welcomed women as members, the Adirondack League Club proudly stating in 1893 that 'Mrs. Nimrod and Mrs. Walton are equally eligible with their husbands.' That mixed hunting parties in the Adirondacks were common was reported by an

English traveler in 1872, who somewhat enviously described the freedom from restraints enjoyed by American girls and women. And although some men were notorious for their building of cabins for 'weekend guests' near their main lodges, Mrs. Hooker claimed such innuendos exaggerated. 'Bachelor' cabins were built for single male guests but were placed at discreet distances from other guest quarters.

William Dix, editor of *Town and Country,* inadvertently described the social life of the Adirondacks while simultaneously arguing that the region's real value was in forestry practices:

> This Adirondack wilderness is notoriously a vast playground for the rich, not merely a haunt for the fisherman and the hunter, not merely an exclusive pleasure preserve where money is lavished in great hotels, elaborate villas and luxurious 'camps,' too far away to be accessible to the general public, but a mighty object lesson in forestry and a source of wealth to the State and country.

Mrs. Brandreth, of the Brandreth Preserve, resting during a hunt in the early 1870s.

Playground and preserve could and did intersect, and the attractions of the wilderness never interfered with the desirability of building camps or joining clubs.

WHEN TRYING to define a 'camp,' one is reminded of Louis Armstrong's famous response to an often repeated question about jazz: 'Man, if you gotta ask, you'll never know.' To some who survived summers away from home under the watchful eyes of counselors, a camp was a refuge from city boredom, pains of adolescence, and shared homesickness. To some, it is a tar paper shack built by their grandfather near a trickle of a stream. And to others, it is a forty-room lodge with a servant and guide for every guest.

Alice M. Kellogg attested to the confusion, writing in *Broadway Magazine* in 1908: 'A camp in the Adirondacks, then, may mean anything from a log fire in the woods to a hundred thousand dollar villa. The only places not called camps are the big hotels where guests dress formally for dinner.' William Dix, gushing enthusiastically about a weekend at a luxurious camp, knew what a camp wasn't: 'An Adirondack camp does not mean a canvas tent or a bark wigwam.' But he also knew that it was distinctive: 'a permanent summer home where the fortunate owners assemble for several weeks each year and live in perfect comfort and even luxury, tho in the heart of the woods, with no near neighbors, no roads and no danger of intrusion.' The Great Camp, as it was termed in the more colorful periods of Adirondack history, meant usually the summer homes of the rich, the luxurious layouts where 'roughing it' was a phrase without much meaning. The New York press and the popular magazines might describe an 'Adirondack hunting lodge,' but the owner always called it a camp.

The private log cabins and tents that grew up around Paul Smith's and other hotels were comfortable, but the most lavish camps were deeper in the woods. As the possession of an elaborate Adirondack hunting lodge became fashionable, the wealthy families looked for remote, isolated places surrounded by hundreds or thousands of private acres of land.

It is generally agreed that the first camps were more or less impromptu constructions. As with the development of other architectural styles, the Great Camps did not spring from any single source. Unspoiled nature, a hunger for greater privacy in the deep woods, ready availability of materials, and ample wealth to command absolute comfort mingled to produce the unique character of the Great Camps. A journalist in 1908 wrote: 'The architectural perfection that is apparent in the Adirondack camps of the finer class is due, in great measure, to the artistic principle of suiting a design to its use and to its situation.'

Great Camps: The Adirondack Style

In the design of a Great Camp, most of the buildings demonstrated a special approach to their wilderness surroundings through deliberate esthetic choices. As one writer described the style: 'Naturally no two are alike; some are elaborate, even to the point of questionable taste. . . . But the truest type is composed of a group of rustic buildings on the edge of a lake, with pathless forests in the rear.'

Of the more prominent elements that can be considered standard features of the Great Camp, the use of log construction, whether true or simulated, is perhaps most striking. While ordinary balloon-frame construction composed the vast majority of country summer homes, logs, though construction was time-consuming and expensive, were laid up as walls, framed as trusses, used as supporting purlins for the roof, and peeled as beams and studs. Every detail possessed structural significance. Extensions of log ends, coping of intersecting logs, and crossbracing of poles became decorative elements.

While the Great Camps surpassed in size and structural complexity the simple log cabins of the early settlers, they conveyed the same sense of shelter from the severe climate, playing on romantic associations with the pioneering spirit and the simple life.

'Rustic work' is another distinctive camp characteristic. A contemporary definition from an architectural dictionary of the period defines the term as:

> decoration by means of rough woodwork, the bark being left in place, or by means of uncut stone, artificial rockwork or the like, or by such combination of these materials and devices as will cause the general appearance of what is thought rural in character. Where woodwork is used it is customary to provide a continuous sheathing as of boards, upon which is nailed the small logs and branches with their bark, moss, etc., carefully preserved.

Rustic shelter at Kamp Kill Kare.

Previously, rustic work was seldom used as architectural ornament, being confined primarily to nineteenth-century garden gazebos and summer houses and their furniture, or to country fences and estate entrance gateways. But in the Adirondacks, roughly dressed limbs and roots of the native trees were used to create imaginative, ornamental patterns, producing unique architectural embellishments. The same skills were applied by the guideboat builders as well, using native materials supplemented by craft, practicality, and some imposed materials. On building exteriors, rustic work included decorative application of peeled-bark sheathing, elaborate branch-work patterns on porch railings, and gable screens. Interiors incorporated it into fireplaces, decorative trim, and all types of imaginative woodland furniture produced on the site.

Another distinguishing feature of Adirondack camps is the tradition of individual buildings for separate functions as permanent buildings replaced tent platforms. Guests were generally lodged in cabins or perhaps on the second floor of the typical lakeside boathouse, separate from the camp owner's living unit. The dining room was often housed in an individual building, while the social gathering place, variously called 'the casino,' the game room, or the trophy lodge, was also a separate unit. Covered boardwalks or enclosed passageways connected the buildings, affording some shelter from the elements.

Separate buildings were particularly well-suited to expansions that continued through successive summers, the camp extending its size with each successive season. As camps grew, they took on the appearance of small settlements. The staff quarters — kitchens, icehouses, barns, workshops, carriage houses, and storerooms — became the service complex, a self-sufficient community in some cases several miles from the main camp.

Advice about building camps was published as early as 1888 by William S. Wicks in *Log Cabins: How to Build and Furnish Them*. Filled with valuable information on selecting a site, construction details and furnishings, plans and sketches, this popular book was published in many editions through the 1920s. Although the book may never have fallen into the hands of the Adirondack guides and local craftsmen, it provided a good primer in basic camp design for the owner or architect. The argument for log construction was set forth simply as a 'civilized' choice: 'The choice of material for a camp is, to a large extent, a matter of taste, expense or convenience. . . . No material equals the log, and no cabin looks so well as the log cabin.' Wick's designs were cabins of log construction, cut from timber on or near the site. Log notching was traditional; windows and doors were set by woodsman's methods; chimneys were of sound, functional design.

Joint framing detail.

In 1931, almost a half century later, Augustus D. Shepard described the transition in camp design in *Camps in the Woods*. As an architect designing Great Camps for several decades at the same Adirondack League Club site as Wicks, Shepard had seen the basic log cabin translated into the elaborate hunting lodge. In Shepard's terms, although his camps were built of logs, they did not have the crude quality (Wicks called it charm), but were in reality 'summer homes in the woods.'

Desirability of a site was based on the available views, access, and a tree-protected waterfront, and, as Wicks said, 'The structure should be the outgrowth of, and harmonize with the site.' Shepard echoes this: 'The buildings must be designed so that they actually appear to grow out of the ground. It should be hardly discernible to the eye where the building commences.'

The most successful Great Camp designs followed the rule that building materials possess certain inherent qualities of the forest. This eliminated such materials as plaster, wallpaper, or paint — either inside or outside the building. The aesthetic point depended on the natural color, figure, and grain of the wood for decorative effects. Spruce, pine, hemlock, tamarack, and balsam were the best for structure; hardwoods were too heavy to handle. Spruce was best for roof boards; pine and spruce for ceilings; pine, spruce, cypress, and gumwood for wall and paneling; and birch, beech, maple, and fir for the floors and stairs.

Fall was the best time of the year to build, with the ground dry and hard, no heavy snows to obstruct the hauling of logs to camp, and bark clinging tightly to the trees. Logs for walls were fastidiously selected for straightness, shape, and taper, and had to be carefully placed to avoid contact with the ground, preventing dry rot. Foundations could

Honnedaga Lodge, a Wicks design for the Adirondack League Club.

take the form of piers or walls, preferably of local stone, although posts of cedar, hemlock, pine, or tamarack placed below frost level could be used instead. Camps like Santanoni, Kill Kare, or Uncas illustrate marvels of craftsmanship, all executed with the woodman's felling axe. In later years, when sawmills were more readily available, it became easier to flatten sides for a tight fit and to slot the length of a log for insertion of hemp weather barriers. But the intricate corner-notching and coping of logs to butt horizontally or at an angle could be done only by skilled workers.

Scholars, fascinated by American log construction, have traced its origins and have categorized different types. Corner-notching is a distinctive feature and is described by Henry Mercer in *The Origin of Log Houses in the United States* (1924), Kniffen and Glassie's *Building in Wood in the Eastern United States* (1966), and others. At least half a dozen types of corner-notching can be found in Adirondack camps, and another half dozen variations of these were used. The saddle notch, dovetail notches (half or full), the 'V' notch, square notches (half or double) were the most common. The familiar 'Lincoln log,' square- or flat-sided, was the double-notch type.

Another highly skilled task was chimney construction. Just getting a fireplace to draw properly and not blow smoke and ash into the room was a difficult task; to make it decorative as well required art. One marvels at the massive hearths at Sagamore and Topridge, large enough to stand in and capped by stone mantles weighing tons. Cyclopean rocks were incorporated into fireplaces at Kill Kare and Nehasane with the apparent ease that ordinary bricklayers show with simpler materials.

The furniture and accessories of a Great Camp added to their character. Wicks urged that 'as far as possible both log cabin and its furniture be made on the spot and with the material at hand.' Beds, chairs, tables, cupboards, and decorative pieces of peeled poles, twigs, and birch bark were works of art, crafted by caretakers and guides over a long winter and presented to an owner upon arrival the following summer. William West Durant developed built-in bench seats, using bent poles polished with beeswax to reveal the natural grain, still fresh in appearance today after almost a century. Under the true craftsman, anonymous at Kamp Kill Kare or known like Ben Muncil, Jr., at Topridge, an interior of rustic furniture blended harmoniously with handrails, lighting fixtures, and the woods of interior surfaces.

An interior at Kamp Kill Kare.

RAQUETTE LAKE, the site of Adirondack Murray's camp, saw an early development of log and bark cabins in the mid-1870s. The arrival of the Durant family, with their plans for developing tourism in the central Adirondacks, focused attention on the lake. William West Durant's simple yet innovative chalet-style camp at Pine Knot caught the attention of Seneca Ray Stoddard.

Only a few modest hunting or fishing cabins existed on Raquette Lake when the Durants first arrived, and his creation, in striking contrast to previous local building, was quickly appreciated as an appropriate architectural model. In 1881, only a few years after Durant began the camp, Stoddard's guidebook hailed Pine Knot as 'unquestionably the most picturesque and recherché affair of its kind in the wilderness.' By 1888 Pine Knot's influence on surrounding camps had become so evident that Stoddard grouped them all together as 'the rustic camps of Raquette Lake.'

During the last two decades of the nineteenth century, the Gilded Age, camp building expanded to the shores of the other central

Great Camps: The Great Expansion

Tent Platforms Become Permanent

Adirondack lakes as well — the St. Regis lakes, Lake Placid, and the Saranac lakes. They may not have been Adirondack hunting lodges in every sense of the phrase, but whatever their degree of purity in Great Camp style, they were durable and often luxurious. Further back in the woods on isolated preserves, the lodges of Pruyn, Webb, Vanderbilt, and others were being built, sometimes in spectacular style.

The St. Regis area saw families like the Stokeses and Reids move from Paul Smith's onto their own sites in the early 1880s. Upper and Lower St. Regis, Spitfire, and Osgood lakes became dotted with clusters of tent platforms separated for different functions: sleeping, dining, staff recreation, and other social activities. Later, the plan was retained as platforms were replaced by permanent buildings, some owners selecting log construction and others using frame structures sheathed with slab siding. The simple boathouse emerged as an important feature of a camp, with slips at water level, rooms for guests or entertainment above, and a broad balcony for a view of lake activities.

Lake Placid was one of the first areas in the Adirondacks to experience extensive camp development. The three or four earliest examples were built around 1872. During the last three decades of the nineteenth century, approximately one hundred camps were built on the lakeshore and islands. This concentrated development resulted in a greater density of smaller camps, most of them conventional summer homes. These differed from their Raquette Lake counterparts, there being only a few examples of the separate-unit plan. The standard Lake Placid camp centralized all functions into one two-story building. The only distinctively rustic element was the use of rough bark siding.

In contrast to Lake Placid, camp building around Saranac Lake came late — at the beginning of the twentieth century. The lake's development was influenced strongly by the establishment of the Adirondack Cottage Sanitorium by Dr. E. L. Trudeau in 1884. In nearby Saranac Lake Village the healthful climate aided the cure of tuberculosis and attracted many who sought fresh mountain air. Large-scale, single-structure summer residences designed by local architect William L. Coulter were popular on Saranac Lake. Conspicuous examples were the immense, German-inspired, half-timbered camps of Adolph Lewisohn and Otto Kahn built during the first decade of the twentieth century.

In this same period, the design trend of the Great Camps shifted from collections of small individual buildings towards an emphasis on main lodges of large size. The compound plan of separate units still continued, but there were generally fewer small buildings and these served as bedroom facilities or guest accommodations. The sophistication of the second- or third-generation summer residence demanded more astute planning in camp building and an expansion of service facilities. Efforts were made to adapt the main lodge to a dramatic site, maintaining privacy for both owner and guests in a single structure with separate support complexes. Camps such as Sagamore, Nehasane, Kill Kare, and Santanoni exemplified this new attitude.

If the first camps were built more or less by inspiration, in time professional architects were called in. Although the versatile guide was adequate for the simple structures of the early camps, as owners sought grand hunting lodges designed in the Adirondack style, professional architectural skill became necessary. In building Santanoni, in 1888, the Pruyn family turned to Robert H. Robertson, and in 1891 William Seward Webb engaged the same architect to design his Forest Lodge at Nehasane Park. The desirability of the rustic log camp, tastefully designed, was illustrated for future Adirondack League Club members in its 1892 prospectus. An attractive two-story cabin, designed by club member Wicks, suggests the rustic as the appropriate architecture. When the era of the 'artistic' cottage came to an end, and owners of preserves and large lakefront holdings insisted upon lavish hunting lodge designs, they turned to a number of prominent architectural firms. These included McKim, Mead, and White; John Russell Pope; and Delano and Aldrich. One New York firm, Davis, McGrath, and Shepard, developed a reputation for its practice in the field of rustic camps during the early 1900s and completed many commissions for the Adirondack League Club.

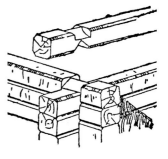

Lock joint framing

Some of the most successful camp designs were by the Saranac Lake architect, William L. Coulter, with later partners Max Westhoff and William G. Distin. The same firm continues today under Arthur Wareham. Owners' requests of the architects were often fabulous. It was Will Distin who was told by one New York client, after approval of a camp design, 'I'm leaving for Europe. I want it built and finished the day I return.' As the camp neared completion the owner cabled, 'Will arrive Thursday. Please buy dishes, and have roast lamb for dinner.' The owner arrived, and as the story goes, china, silver, flowers, and roast lamb were on the table.

The architects who designed Great Camps received widespread national attention through the publication of drawings, plans, and photographs in architectural journals and popular magazines. In 1916 the newly formed National Park Service adopted the style for lodges and camps; thus, places like Yellowstone, Glacier Park, and Jackson Hole have fine examples of rustic architecture. Eventually, rustic details were incorporated into design standards of the vast national public works programs of the Depression years. A generation of landscape architects were trained and employed in the use of rustic work. But the beginnings of the style were on Raquette Lake with the work of William West Durant, barely a decade after the end of the Civil War.

69

CHAPTER 5

DURANT: THE MAN AND HIS CAMPS

Thomas C. Durant's camp on Long Point, 1877 or 1878

THE HISTORY of tourism in the central Adirondacks during the last quarter of the nineteenth century is in large part the story of William West Durant. He was born in Brooklyn in 1850, scion of the railroad builder, Thomas C. Durant. When the famous steamship *Great Eastern* made her first Atlantic crossing in 1861, eleven-year-old William was a passenger, bound for a European education. Except for a few months' visit home in 1866, he remained abroad, studying in England and Germany and traveling extensively. In his early twenties, William became interested in exploring the Middle East. He was in Egypt in 1874 when called home by his father to help in developing the central Adirondacks.

The son's projects, accomplished over the next twenty-five years, are unparalleled in the history of the Adirondacks.

Donaldson sums up the career of W. W. Durant:

> He succeeded his father as president of the Adirondack Railroad, and carried on his many development schemes with an enthusiasm born of a genuine delight in the woods. He added whole townships to his inherited land holdings; he built the first artistic camps the woods had ever seen, and opened up the Raquette Lake region by facilities of transportation unknown before. Indeed, he was conspicuously the developer of the central Adirondacks. From 1885 to 1900 he enjoyed an unrivalled regency of prominence and popularity. He entertained largely and royally, and made a name for himself as a pioneer woodland host. He was the first to make his summer quarters comfortable for winter pleasures, and to use them for that purpose. He was the first to ask his friends to travel north by train and then by sleigh over forty miles of snow and ice for the novelty of eating Christmas dinner in the wilderness. He was, in short, the first to inaugurate many things which had never been dreamed of in the Adirondacks before.

Upon his arrival at Raquette Lake in 1876, the son went to work on the father's plans for opening the central Adirondacks for tourism. The rigorous trip from the railhead at North Creek to Raquette Lake had to be improved to bring tourists to the central Adirondacks. A transportation system was planned linking the thirty miles from North Creek to Blue Mountain Lake by a stagecoach line. For the twelve-mile distance to Raquette Lake, he established a line of rowboats, later replacing them with several steamboats. At the same time, William's cousin Frederick, son of Charles W. Durant, came to build the Prospect House on Blue Mountain Lake. Setting aside his plans for hotels and clubs, William West Durant broke ground on his personal residence. In the summer of 1877 the elder Durant had built two or three simple one-story cabins on Long Point. During the building, one of the family had found a remarkable, three-foot-wide pine knot shaped like the hilt of a sword, which was quickly adopted as the camp totem. When William took over Camp Pine Knot in 1878, he gradually transformed the original, featureless buildings into 'artistic' cabins of Swiss chalet lines. Pine Knot grew and evolved, ultimately becoming a cluster of buildings, large and small, connected and detached.

Durant built hunting camps on other holdings — south of Raquette Lake on Shedd and Sumner lakes and on Rich and Arbutus lakes in Essex County. His development schemes went forward, including camps, elegant hotels and golf courses, and modern transportation. Telegraph lines were strung into the region to bring the latest word from the outside. The line of rowboats along the Fulton Chain was replaced by a fleet of steamboats, the largest holding two hundred passengers.

Not discouraged by Webb's Utica–Montreal line bypassing Blue Mountain Lake, Durant planned for a Pullman sleeping car in regular service between Grand Central Station and the Eckford Chain. To connect the steamboat line running from Raquette Lake to the end of the Marion River across a three-quarter-mile portage, Durant built the world's shortest standard-gauge railroad. It was six miles from the nearest tracks of any other line and equipped with open horse-drawn cars purchased from the Brooklyn Rapid Transit Company. The cars cost twenty-five dollars apiece and were hooked up to an oil-burning converted steam locomotive.

Marion River Carry train.

Although the Pullman Company refused to risk an expensive car on a winding Adirondack stream, the line carried eight thousand to ten thousand passengers a year, as well as freight, from 1900 until it was abandoned in 1929. Durant relished the tradition among railroaders that enabled him to use the railroad letterhead to secure passes from major lines across the country in exchange for the privilege of a twelve-mile ride in a small steamboat followed by a three-quarter-mile ride in a former horse car.

In the midst of his plans Durant was suddenly sued by his sister for the mishandling of his father's estate. Since his father's death, he had been living on a lavish scale, spending far more on building his camps and carrying out his land development and transportation schemes than his actual income covered. As he once told Harold Hochschild, 'I was handicapped, by having been brought up in wealth without being taught the value of money.' His sister's lawsuit in 1891 was followed by divorce proceedings by his wife, Janet L. Stott, daughter of a Raquette Lake neighbor, in 1896.

Durant decided to defy his sister and carry out his plans. In order to raise cash he began to sell some of his properties. Collis P. Huntington, builder of the Central Pacific and Southern Pacific railroads, was interested in Durant's plans and had taken a liking to the young man. In 1895 he purchased Pine Knot from Durant. Durant moved to a new camp he had started in 1890 at Sumner Lake — Camp Uncas — and then sold it to J. P. Morgan in 1896. He next moved on to Sagamore Lodge, which he was building for himself and his mother. By 1900 he was deep in debt, and counted on his friend Huntington to help him out. Huntington arrived in the Adirondacks that summer but a few days later died of a heart attack at Camp Pine Knot.

Huntington's death ended Durant's great dream, for the estate's executors would not honor the deceased's promises. Morgan, Webb, and Whitney heirs also turned down his entreaties, viewing Durant as fiscally irresponsible. In 1901, he sold Sagamore to Alfred G. Vanderbilt. Judgments favoring his sister were followed by foreclosures on his land companies and his transportation companies. By 1904 Durant was bankrupt.

Although he lived for another thirty years, he regained neither affluence nor prominence. A happy remarriage in 1906 enabled him to weather his reduced circumstances. In 1907 and 1908 he returned to the Adirondacks, managing hotels at Long Lake and Newcomb, often serving the men he had once employed. Two years after his death in 1934, the state named a man-made lake after him; a bronze memorial plaque was fixed to a boulder on the roadside by Durant Lake a mile from Blue Mountain Village. But there is another memorial much greater. He was a builder ahead of his time. His camps, with a special

*Durant's
Misfortunes*

quality of utility, fitness, and beauty, influenced the creation of the Adirondack style. Harold Hochschild, one of Durant's great admirers, eulogizes him:

> He foresaw, perhaps more clearly than anyone else, the need to make the [central Adirondacks] better known and easier of approach, and he did much to bring that about. Hundreds of thousands of visitors who have found pleasure in this region during the past half century, most of whom never heard of William West Durant, have had reason to be grateful to him.

Although the undercurrents of an emerging, indigenous rustic style existed when Durant first came to the heart of the Adirondack wilderness in the 1870s, it was his creation of a harmonious woodland architecture that largely inspired and institutionalized the style as we know it today. Durant's simple design took the best features of the Adirondack early log cabin and combined them with the decorative features of the long, low Swiss chalet, making a building style that blended perfectly with a woodland or lakeshore setting.

Left, *'W.W.D.,' with rustic gable and fan at Camp Pine Knot.* Below, *Thomas C. Durant's log cabin rebuilt by his son as the 'Chalet.'*

*William West Durant
at Camp Pine Knot.*

William Chapman White describes Durant's invention:

> The idea of Swiss influence, so common in decoration, in
> gables, balconies, and other details copied later in the
> Adirondack camps, may have been something Durant re-
> membered from his travels in Europe. It may also have
> come consciously or unconsciously from an Adirondack
> building that preceded Pine Knot in its use of Swiss orna-
> mentation along with gables, verandahs, and similar fea-
> tures. This was the Wayside Hotel at Lake Luzerne, which
> Durant knew.

The style is as much borrowed as it is indigenous; conditions of terrain, weather, and available materials are similar in the northern timbered region of Alpine countries, and in Scandinavia, Russia, and
Japan. Examples of Swiss chalet decoration and building methods,
Japanese structural techniques and ornamentation, Russian dachas,
and Bavarian details can be found at various locations. Camp owners
themselves introduced foreign styles encountered on travels abroad
and on visits to international expositions. Part of Adirondack folklore
is the story told by Hochschild of William West Durant's leaving a
Swiss music box with his superintendent at Eagle's Nest, requesting
that it be used as a model for his own residence.

But it was Durant's work that was to determine the fundamentals of Adirondack camp architecture. Donaldson described the quintessential camp, Pine Knot:

> This was the first of the artistic and luxurious camps. . . . It was a unique blend of beauty and of comfort. It was the showplace of the woods. Men took a circuitous route in order to gain a glimpse of it, and to have been a guest within its timbered walls and among its woodland fancies was to wear the hall-mark of the envied. Before it was built there was nothing like it; since then, despite infinite variations, there has been nothing essentially different from it.

In Durant's four camps — Pine Knot, Uncas, and Sagamore, a few miles south of Raquette Lake, and the adjacent Kamp Kill Kare — the significant elements of the Great Camp are all present: log construction; rustic treatment of decorative work and furniture; and self-sufficient, multibuilding complexes. Other camps, built by the Whitneys, Carnegies, Vanderbilts, Colliers, Morgans, and Huntingtons, are all marked by the influence of Durant.

Camp Pine Knot

LONG POINT in Raquette Lake is a peninsula running east and west, roughly two miles long and a half mile wide. Thomas C. Durant's first campsite was on the north shore of the tip of the point. When his son took over, he chose a more attractive site on the southwest tip of Long Point amid giant white pines. Starting in 1879, Pine Knot's main chalet was conceived as the central image of the new camp complex.

The Pine Knot buildings have an affinity with the chalets of the Bernese Oberland, with their characteristic second-floor galleries under the projecting eaves of a broad, low roof. However, the importance of European precedents in the eventual development of the style of the Great Camps should not be overemphasized. It may be that similarities in weather conditions prompted the adoption of certain features such as the gradual roof slope designed to retain thick accumulations of snow as insulation.

An important concept of Durant's design realized in Pine Knot is the use of structure as a decorative element. The collar beam and truss of the front gable, the exposed ribs that carry the roof, and the corbeling of projecting beams that support the upper story are examples of structural elements that are also intrinsic parts of the building's aesthetic image. Durant's main lodge and later buildings at Pine Knot, Uncas, and Sagamore were constructed of spruce logs taken from the site, joined by corner-lock joints in which notches were carved in the bottom of the log only. In contrast to the typical double-notch method

At Camp Pine Knot, Durant's simple tent-like structures of logs or cedar bark sheathing were constructed with craftsmanship. Porches and bay windows were added to the basic forms, with rustic work or decorative devices — such as the pine knot that provided the camp's name.

of frontier buildings, the craftsmanship in the lodge was comparatively sophisticated.

Fully aware that lumber was available from nearby sawmills, Durant still selected log construction over conventional framing systems, a deliberate aesthetic decision. His demand for quality workmanship was answered by skilled guides who found occupational versatility necessary for Adirondack survival. Durant's insistence on perfect construction is described in the *Encyclopedia of American Biography:*

> He would have his men search for days for timber with just the grain of texture which polished, would best adorn some feature of a house. In stone work the cut or broken side must not show, only that which showed in nature. While building a wall eight feet high for a lodge, he was called to New York for a conference with Collis P. Huntington. When he returned he found that a workman had put in one stone with a cut side out. He had the whole wall taken down to correct the mistake. He could take the native wood, polish it and treat it with a beeswax preparation so that its sweet scent stayed for generations.

Nearly all of the camp units at Pine Knot demonstrated creativity, ingenuity, and craftsmanship; all used natural materials from the camp

Building details at Camp Pine Knot.

surroundings. Unpeeled limbs and branches of cedar or spruce were converted into ornamental porch railings and gable screens. An entire structure was given a rustic appearance by sheets of peeled cedar bark applied as sheathing over frame construction, with accents of split poles applied around doors and windows. Although leaving the bark on logs was aesthetically important, special applications of stains and preservatives were required to discourage insect borers. Durant extended the use of intricate rustic work to interiors, using birch bark to cover walls or ceilings, constructing unique fireplaces from stones found on the site, and designing rustic furniture for his craftsmen to build.

In his Adirondack guidebook of 1889, Seneca Ray Stoddard described the salient features of the Raquette Lake Camps:

> The camps of Raquette Lake are elegant affairs, and although built of rustic material found ready to the hand, it is apparent that twisted cedar, shaggy spruce and silvery birch, in their native vestments, were not chosen because they cost nothing there. Some of these camps are works of art, and filled with dainty bric-a-brac; generally however, pertaining to woodsy things, and in keeping with their native environment. The pioneer camp of this section and of the most artistic in the woods, is 'Camp Pine Knot' on the South Bay.

Rustic work required craftsmanship in selecting and assembling natural materials. Success in application of the style depended upon the skills of the native workmen and the patience and money of the owner.

The organic form of the Pine Knot complex was the result of ongoing planning and building over successive seasons. Stoddard explained this trait in his 1888 guidebook: 'These camps are *never* really completed, for one of the fascinating features of the camp is that it is bound by no rules of time and architecture. It expands and blossoms with the passing seasons.'

By the time Durant sold the camp to Huntington, Pine Knot resembled a small community. One of the most unusual structures was a bark cabin built on a raft of pine logs and moored near the boathouse. The *Barque,* as it was called, was built as a floating refuge from the black flies. Measuring twenty feet wide and sixty feet long, the houseboat had four rooms, a kitchen, bath, and running water. In preparing for the sale to Huntington, Durant's 1895 inventory included:

1 Swiss Cottage containing 7 rooms with open fireplace
1 Log Cottage and annex containing bedroom, dressing room, stove room and bathroom with open fireplace
1 Double Frame Cottage containing 3 bedrooms, with open fireplace
1 Log Cottage containing 3 rooms
1 Log Cottage consisting of one room with open fireplace
1 Double Frame Cottage containing 3 rooms and bathroom with two open fireplaces
1 Frame Cottage containing 5 rooms (guide's house)
1 Frame Building containing kitchen, pantry, store room and servant's dining room
1 Woodshed
1 Glass dining room
1 Ice House with meat cooler
1 Large Frame Building containing 3 rooms and one dark closet; used to store boats, carpenter's shop, store room and photographic room
1 Water Tank Building
1 Wood Shop
1 Pump House
1 Boat House
1 Laundry and Laundry store room
2 Open Camps
1 Stone Ash House
1 Covered Shed
1 Small outdoor dressing room for bathers
2 Potato Cellars
1 Horse Barn (5 stall), wagon shed, cow-shed
1 Hot Frame
1 Dog Yard — dog kennel

Camp Pine Knot, built in 1879, photographed in 1979.

The many buildings on the site were scattered in an informal manner, each separate from the next. Sites were selected for views, and within general proximity of each other for convenience of moving about in bad weather.

Durant's compound plan did not contain or define exterior space as did the functional structures of forested lands in northern Europe, Russia, or Japan. The scheme reflected the character of temporary woodsmen's or guides' camps, more or less random groupings of tent platforms. Rather than tack a new wing onto an existing structure to incorporate a new function, it was preferred to construct an entirely separate structure.

There were also practical reasons for the compound-plan tradition. A greater degree of privacy was afforded by the separated structures; at the same time, the sense of community, important in an isolated forest location, was provided by an extended complex. The separation of units also afforded a measure of fire protection. Building locations were selected for ease of siting, views, exposures, and accommodation to the terrain. Walkways between buildings, infinite in their variety and degree of sophistication, subtly created closer contact with the outdoors. Nature could sometimes be too close for comfort, however, and so Durant introduced covered walkways extending from the building porches as protection against persistent Adirondack drizzles.

The fate of Camp Pine Knot has been happier than the fates of Durant and Huntington. The camp stood empty for almost half a century until it was presented to the State University of New York College at Cortland in January 1949. Renamed the Huntington Memorial Outdoor Education Center, the camp has thrived under the direction of Dr. George Fuge. Durant had constructed the buildings so well that only modest repairs were required and, under Dr. Fuge's direction, restoration work has continued, including rebuilding of the *Barque*. Thousands of students and guests have enjoyed the camp over the past three decades, a fine example of the potential for adaptive reuse of Great Camps.

Camp Uncas

WHILE BUILDING Camp Pine Knot on Raquette Lake, Durant kept his eye on prospective purchasers of his land holdings. The budding real estate promoter took guests on hunting and fishing trips deep in the woods, staying overnight in lean-tos or bark shanties built by his guides. But this was hardly the way to attract the wealthy — who were first introduced to the Adirondacks by the comforts of Camp Pine Knot. In the 1880s, turning his attention south of Raquette Lake to three small lakes, Durant built two hunting lodges for himself, one at Sumner Lake and the other at Shedd Lake. Transporting men and ma-

Opposite, *Camp Uncas,
Durant's second venture for
his personal use.*
Top, *Camp Uncas boat-
house of simple pole barn
structure.*
Middle, *The dining room
building at Camp Uncas.*
Bottom, *Pine Knot's fragile
tent platform buildings
were transformed by Durant
into more robust forms at
Camp Uncas.*

terials six miles by road cut through the woods, he directed the building of the lodges with logs felled on the sites.

In 1890 Durant shifted his activities to the third lake, Mohegan. Here he started building a second permanent summer home, Camp Uncas. 'On the shores of this tiny, toy-like lake in the deepest depths of the forest,' writes Donaldson, 'Mr. Durant built a most wonderful camp in 1890. Owing to its utter isolation it was seldom seen and but little known, and yet it was more massively beautiful and more cunningly luxurious than even Pine Knot.' The spot Durant picked had no navigable access; the only entry was via a private dirt road through dense forest. Hochschild described the rigors of constructing on remote sites typical of many of the Great Camps.

> The sawed timbers for these [window] frames were carried in from Raquette Lake, six miles through the woods, by two men in tandem. On each man's shoulders rested a sap-yoke, similar to the yokes used in carrying guide boats. The timbers were suspended in slings of rope hung from the ends of each yoke, three timbers on each side.

In contrast to Pine Knot's extended thirteen-year building period, Uncas was completed in two.

The brief building period did not mean Durant reduced the number of structures. Even though Uncas was massive and luxurious, the compound plan developed at Pine Knot was retained. Most of the buildings were designed with a multifunctional approach.

For the camp's main lodge, Durant chose native logs as the major building material. Interestingly, the framing system was not true log construction, for instead of lock joints with the typical alternating projections of vertically cut ends, the lodge's spruce logs were diagonally hewn to dovetail and form mitered joints. An uncommon technique at the time, this system structurally depended upon the careful setting of drift pins into the end of the logs to secure them. Again, the choice of logs was a deliberate, aesthetic decision, crucial to the overall design of the camp. Although only two of Uncas's buildings are of true log construction, the use of log siding and other natural materials produces harmonious forms. At Uncas, Durant may have been experimenting in different types of construction for future camp projects. Two lakeside cottages are conventional frame buildings with bark siding over plank sheathing. On other bark-sheathed cabins, massive split logs were placed vertically between windows, details more ponderous than those at Pine Knot. The log framing of the main boathouse was bolder than anything at the earlier Raquette Lake camp, showing a greater confidence in using large logs, coped and joined precisely. The enterprising use of materials was continued in an icehouse and a store-room with foundation walls of cyclopean rock, a technique used later at neighboring Kamp Kill Kare.

The dining building, using log construction similar to that of the main lodge was modified by Anne Morgan, daughter of Uncas's purchaser. About twenty-four by thirty-six feet in plan, the building was a simple tent form, twelve feet to the eaves. The roof ridge was more than twenty feet above the floor, with peeled log beams supporting smooth-finished plank ceilings. A massive fireplace presided at one end of the room; panels of fully glazed doors on the opposite end and sides flooded the room with natural light.

The rustic work at Uncas is less elaborate than at Pine Knot. The original novelty seems to have palled for Durant, perhaps because so many camps of the 1880s and 1890s copied or enlarged upon Pine Knot's examples. Uncas's stepped-up building schedule may also have had its effect, although craftsmanship was hardly neglected during construction; for instance, all the buildings' iron hardware was made in a blacksmith's shop on the site. Log work and use of local stone for exteriors and interiors were executed exceedingly well throughout. Moreover, the built-in furnishing and furniture are the most innovative rustic work in the camp.

The dining room at Camp Uncas.

Sagamore Lodge was Durant's last camp-building venture. Opposite, *seen from the air, the main lodge is sited on a peninsula jutting into the lake. The bowling alley extends across the bottom of the photograph.* Above left, *bark sheathing covers the walls of a guest cabin.* Above right, *original cabins were expanded and interconnected with covered walkways.* Left, *the main lodge was a log-covered, framed chalet, housing thirty guests.* Below, *the service compound was a mile from the family compound.*

Dining room and main living room at Camp Uncas with finished surfaces of polished plank and peeled logs, and superbly fitted stone fireplaces. Built-in banquettes of burnished and scented wood were complemented by wrought ironwork fabricated on the site.

The interiors of Uncas conveyed a subtle rustic atmosphere. Although certainly not as finished as those of conventional summer homes, the rooms still exhibited extraordinary refinement. The rough natural bark, stripped away in favor of peeled and polished surfaces, revealed the beauty of the native woods. Floors, walls, and ceilings of polished planking and peeled log beams glowed warmly in the main camp buildings. The masculine hunting-lodge motif so characteristic of later Great Camps also made its appearance at Uncas: taxidermy specimens ranging from mounted deer heads to bear-skin rugs appeared everywhere. The distinctive interior masonry fireplaces, each of a different design, are unequaled in the Adirondacks.

Durant's enjoyment of Camp Uncas was short-lived. Having sold Pine Knot in 1895 to Huntington for ready cash, Durant again found himself pressed by his creditors. He lived at Uncas during its construction but sold it to J. Pierpont Morgan in 1896. The selling price is not known, but Durant said that the camps and nearby farm alone cost him $120,000. A preserve of 1100 acres and Lake Mohegan went with the sale. Morgan used the camp infrequently, but he thoroughly enjoyed his visits. Immediately after taking over the camp he financed construction of an eight-and-a-half-mile winter road from the Big Moose Station on the New York Central to Eagle Bay, and journeyed the first winter by sleigh to Uncas. Durant used the camp with Morgan's approval from time to time to entertain political guests.

After Morgan's death in 1913 the camp passed to his children and their heirs, until it was sold in 1947 to Mrs. Vanderbilt, owner of the neighboring Sagamore Lodge. It was mentioned in the press in August 1949, when General and Mrs. George Marshall, guests of the owner, entertained Madame Chiang Kai-shek.

After years of hard use as a Boy Scout camp, Uncas, was purchased for private use in 1975. Because of its remote location and guarded entrances, the camp has had far less exposure than Pine Knot on Raquette Lake. It was seldom mentioned in guidebooks; other than in rare publications in 1904, photographs were not published until the early 1950s. Though well-conceived and firmly built, Uncas is overshadowed by Durant's supreme achievement only two miles away: Camp Sagamore.

Sagamore Lodge

HEAVY DEBTS and the forced sale of Pine Knot and Uncas did not deter Durant from embarking on yet another camp. Conceived as his year-round home, Sagamore Lodge was started in late 1896 on the site of an earlier hunting camp. South of Raquette Lake and adjacent to Uncas and Kamp Kill Kare, Shedd Lake (renamed Sagamore by Durant) is a three-hundred-acre rectangle fed by mountain streams. When Durant first purchased the property for his farm and camp buildings, tall white pines covered the site and crowded the lake's shore. He selected a dramatic point of high ground on a peninsula jutting from the southwest shore of the lake; by the summer of 1897 he had moved with his mother into the newly-completed main lodge.

Like Durant's earlier camps, Sagamore was designed on the compound plan. Service structures were grouped a half-mile from the main buildings. But there is a new boldness in the Sagamore site design, the distance among buildings and larger size of structures testifying to Durant's increased expertise.

The Sagamore main lodge is one of the most impressive Great Camp buildings. The Swiss influence is more evident than at Pine Knot or Uncas, although the proportions of a typical chalet were expanded to an immense three-and-a-half stories. Overall dimensions of the ground floor alone were 76 by 104 feet. Although not a true log cabin — it is a frame structure sheathed with half-round spruce logs — the building displays an interesting blend of rustic details. Some elements common to log construction include projecting roof rafters and beams between the first and second floors. While not structural, the projecting logs communicate the strong, masculine image Durant sought. The rustic character is sustained in the porch railings, massive wrought-iron hardware, and peeled-log brackets and window frames.

The oversized structural components of the main lodge were repeated in the boathouses, bowling alleys, woodsheds, and other freestanding buildings. Their construction clearly reveals the interconnectedness of the basic structural elements, using intersections of framing as a decorative device. Later Great Camps created by architects in the region display similar treatments in gable fans.

The interior of Sagamore's main lodge was the most refined of Durant's three camps. Here he provided a showplace for luxurious accoutrements that only great wealth could afford. But the real genius of the interior was that even while conveying an atmosphere of prepossessing prosperity, it simultaneously expressed the recognizable motifs of rusticity. The lodge's main room contained round, polished ceiling beams; walls and ceilings were finished with wide tongue-and-groove pine planks. Bedrooms on the main floor had similar details, using pine planking for floors and narrow polished wainscoting with a burlap covering above on walls. Every room contained a stone fireplace with a full complement of wrought-iron andirons and hardware forged on the site. Oriental rugs and assorted animal hides covered the wide-plank pine floors.

Living room,
Sagamore Lodge.

Between 1898 and 1901 Durant added several other buildings to the camp: a little laundry and dining room, a small boathouse, a stable, and a floating observation post on the lake. The indefatigable architect had set out to build his last lodge with three goals in mind: to prove that summer quarters could be made comfortable for winter use and pleasure; to be the first to invite friends for Christmas dinner in an isolated winter setting; and to be acknowledged the greatest host and entertainer in the Adirondacks. He succeeded on all three counts, but enjoyed the pleasures of Sagamore for less than four years.

Faced again with imminent bankruptcy, Durant liquidated the Sagamore property in 1901, and sold the camp to Alfred G. Vanderbilt. Claiming the camp cost $250,000 to build, Durant valued it at $200,000. He received only $162,500 for the buildings and land.

Vanderbilt married Elsie French in 1901 and honeymooned at Sagamore. Improvements were added — an underground water and sewer system, and a nursery called Lakeside Cabin for the Vanderbilt children and their guests.

His first marriage having ended in divorce, Vanderbilt married Margaret Emerson McKim in 1908. Building resumed at Sagamore. A private pullman coach, the 'Wayfarer,' was purchased to make the journey from New York to Raquette Lake more comfortable. The entrance road was rebuilt and Vanderbilt had local craftsmen build two elegant carriages, drawn by matched teams of four horses, to carry guests from the village to Sagamore.

William Coulter of Saranac Lake designed a gem of a building, the 'Amusement Hall,' for the Vanderbilts in 1901, incorporating in a single space the finest evocation of Durant's ideas. Coulter planned the building along the lines and feeling of the main lodge. Originally intended as the children's playroom, it was converted by Vanderbilt into a game room for exhibiting the family fishing and hunting trophies. The building is a single large room, fifty by sixty feet, open to the ceiling and with a verandah ten feet wide. Peeled and polished logs, plank floors, beamed ceilings carried on trusses, and exposed planking recall Durant's earlier work at Uncas and Pine Knot. A massive fireplace is centered on one end wall, with built-in banquette seating located along the other walls. The wrought-iron hardware and fireplace accessories, and a chandelier of exquisite craftsmanship, were made on the site. The staff taxidermist had his office in the rear and the walls were covered with his work.

Expansion of the camp stopped for a period after Vanderbilt was drowned in the sinking of the *Lusitania* in 1915. Building resumed with Mrs. Vanderbilt's remarriage in 1918. In 1924 Vanderbilt's widow decided the dining room needed enlarging. She drew a square in the dirt and told the caretaker, 'This is something like what I want.' By

Sagamore Lodge's dining room, expanded in 1924 to seat seventy-five guests.

Christmas a building one hundred fifty by thirty feet, including a dining room to seat seventy-five, a kitchen, a pantry, and a gun room, were completed for the annual holiday party.

Through another divorce and remarriage, Vanderbilt's widow, Mrs. Margaret Emerson, continued the expansion of Sagamore. Cottages were added for the children, George, Gloria, and Alfred, and eventually the camp grew to the size of two entire villages, one for family and guests, the other to house the staff and support services. Ninety-nine guests could sleep comfortably in the forty-six bedrooms, and wash in twenty-three bathrooms. In the ten permanent buildings there were twenty-eight fireplaces, each of individual design.

By the late 1920s Sagamore had acquired a national reputation as one of the country's most beautiful woodland camps. It stood for fifty years as an elite wilderness rendezvous for American High Society, sharing with Topridge the cachet of being the only Adirondack camp to be featured in *Life* magazine. Guests included politicians, financiers, entertainers, and celebrities, among them General Pershing, Lord Mountbatten, Averell Harriman, George C. Marshall, Gary Cooper, Gene Tierney, Jean Arthur, Eddy Duchin, and Bernard Baruch.

Local storytellers insist that Hoagy Carmichael wrote his famous song 'Stardust' while driving a beat-up Model A Ford on the dirt road to Sagamore.

The fate of Sagamore typifies the dilemma facing the Great Camps. In 1954, Mrs. Emerson gave the camp to Syracuse University, which operated it as a conference center for twenty years. But after twenty years, escalating maintenance costs made this arrangement impossible. An offer was made, but use of the land would have been incompatible with the adjacent forest preserve lands and the New York Department of Environmental Conservation offered to purchase the property. State acquisition, however, would necessitate demolition of the Great Camp buildings, in accordance with Article XIV, the 'forever wild' provision, of the state constitution. A last-minute reprieve was inveigled by an ad-hoc committee of the Preservation League of New York State in order to seek a buyer for that portion of the land encompassing the major structures. The League, acquiring title to the buildings and a small parcel of land, solicited prospective purchasers in an effort to resell the camp. Restrictive covenants in the deed were designed to discourage speculative offers. These covenants included the first option to purchase at the original price in the event of resale, periodic inspection by the League, and repurchase rights at the original price if, after a two-year period, maintenance was unsatisfactory. Other conditions included the right of public access at regularly scheduled times, and prohibition of alcoholic beverages in the camp or the use of motorboats on the lake. A buyer consenting to all these restrictions was finally found acceptable to the League and the Department, and the sale was completed.

Unfortunately, the furnishings of Sagamore were not included in the transaction, for the state was not interested in acquiring the buildings' contents. An auction dispersed the furnishings, furniture, trophies, and memorabilia so integral to the camp. A prize purchase was the collection of scarlet blankets with trim of black stripes, monogrammed with a flowing 'W.W.D.,' the last remnants of Durant's brief presence at the greatest of his Raquette Lake camps. Now a private conference center, the camp is open to the public on summer weekends.

CHAPTER 6

RAQUETTE LAKE AREA

Camp Fairview on Osprey Island

N 1877, when the Durants settled on Long Point at Raquette Lake, their only summer neighbor was a camp on the southeast shore. By 1900, the area had an impressive collection of Great Camps built in Durant's rustic style. The similarities among these camps can be attributed in part to the limited number of craftsmen and builders working in the area, and the versatile Adirondack guides, rather than the camp owners, may have been the ones responsible for developing the particularly appealing decorative and construction techniques. By incorporating these select elements, many of Raquette Lake's early wood-frame summer homes or log hunting cabins were transformed into elegant Great Camps.

Three camps built in the area in the early 1880s are of interest because they represent Durant's influence, the skill of local craftsmen, and contemporary trends in American architecture. They are also important steps in the evolution of camp architecture from Durant's small-scale structures to the massive lodges built soon after 1900. One of the first camps to show the influence of Pine Knot was Camp Fairview, built in the autumn of 1880 on Osprey Island by a cousin, C. W. Durant, Jr. Although little evidence of the original camp now remains, photographs by Seneca Ray Stoddard and Edward Bierstadt record its design. At the same time, the Durant cousin, Frederick, began a camp known as The Cedars on Forked Lake, a northern tributary of Raquette Lake. The camp was demolished by a later owner in the mid-1950s, but fortunately it too was recorded by Stoddard and Bierstadt in its early days, and again by Margaret Bourke-White in the 1930s. A third camp, known as Echo Point Camp, was begun on Raquette Lake in 1883 by Phineas Lounsbury, a former governor of Connecticut. Still standing, it remains in an excellent state of preservation.

The three camps, almost identical in massing of the main buildings and detail of log construction, exhibit the transition from early hotels and cabins in the Raquette Lake area to Durant's Pine Knot. They were multibuilding camps with rustic exterior work used sparingly although interiors displayed rich imagination in furnishings and decor. These camps followed trends in American architecture emerging, in Vincent Scully's phrase, as the 'stick style.' Rather than a collection of spaces fitted to conform to a floor plan in a single building, individual spaces — such as dining rooms, bedrooms, or libraries — were expressed as distinct, bold forms by grouping them in separate buildings.

In addition to this innovation, the broad verandah that was becoming a common feature of Victorian hotels and domestic buildings was integrated into the overall Adirondack aesthetic by extending the gables. This projection of logs and roof overhangs was functional as well, though it was less adventurously applied at Fairview than at The Cedars and Echo Camp.

Another distinctive technique of the style was to 'float' the buildings free of the ground, the massive foundation logs resting on single boulders or short columns. Rustic skirting prevented the entry of animals beneath the building, but allowed the free movement of air, which kept the building dry during long spells of vacancy. This technique appears in the early hotels and in Durant's other camps, and may have been introduced by local craftsmen as a solution for nonwinterized buildings.

A characteristic Durant detail incorporated into the three camps was the method of framing window and door openings. Unpeeled logs three to four inches in diameter were used to define the openings. Vertical posts were then coped into the horizontal pieces, providing a change in scale from the massive horizontal logs to the hinged casement windows. Window frames usually were given a coat of red gloss paint.

Camp Fairview

The suggestion that architects were instrumental in the design of these earliest camps is plausible, for there are certainly distinct similarities among them and they are consistent with design movements then current in American architecture. Andrew Jackson Downing's innovations in the mid-nineteenth century (*The Architecture of Country Houses*, 1850) foreshadowed the stick style. During the period between Downing's death in 1851 and the Philadelphia Centennial Exposition of 1876 when the style flourished, American domestic architecture was breaking away from the grand styles of the past and absorbing influences from the comparable wooden styles of Switzerland and Japan. With his pattern books, Andrew Jackson Downing and those writers who followed him formulated theories that insisted upon 'truthfulness' in wooden construction, emphasizing function and the nature of materials, picturesque massing, and free-form invention. Guides such as *Palliser's Model Homes for the People* (Bridgeport, 1876) and Pierce and Dockstader's *Modern Building at Moderate Costs* (Elmira, 1886) offered designs, house plans, illustrative construction details, and cost estimates. Asymmetrical, free in form, and varied in massing, the plans disseminated by the pattern books were distinguished by the articulation of wooden members and the emphasis on structural and visual multiplication of the framing.

Whether or not Camp Fairview, The Cedars, or Echo Camp were in fact designed by architects cannot be determined. But there is little doubt that they all shared the same influences that had reached their owners from exposure to this American domestic architecture. What matters most is that, in these three camps, the Adirondack style is established as a unique vernacular architecture. Construction is solid and expressive precisely because building resources were limited. Form largely depended on the lengths of available logs, the basic building blocks, that had to be either cut on site or transported across the lakes and through surrounding forests. Thus each element — walls, the compact massing, and the sheltering roof with its protective over-hang — grew from actual need. A romantic rationalism perhaps, but whatever it is called, it correctly identifies the fusion of architectural reality and rustic aesthetic of the Great Camps.

THE FIRST of the camps, Fairview, was started on Osprey Island in 1880 and took three years to complete. For a short while, the island was named Murray's Island after the famous minister-author who set up a camp there in 1869. The hermit-guide Alvah Dunning took over the campsite for a few years before the 'crowds' of tourists forced him out.

As seen in photographs of the early 1880s, Stoddard's from the north and Beirstadt's from the south, the main lodge consists of a central one-story hall flanked by two-story block buildings. The distinctive profile of a central low-ridge roof is balanced symmetrically by the two higher ridge roofs against the towering white pines on the shore line. Main-building forms are complemented by the attached porches, balconies, and railings of peeled logs.

Fairview's other buildings, guest cottages, staff quarters, and boat-house, are executed in exteriors of unpeeled spruce. The transition

Camp Fairview

Charles W. Durant's main lodge at Camp Fairview.

from lumber-framed building to log construction is most evident in the treatment of exterior building corners. Unlike Durant's use of projecting notched logs, at Fairview vertical timbers at the corners receive butted horizontal logs. This required precise cutting to fit between corner posts and to avoid notching and coping of corner logs. Whether this was due to the unavailability of craftsmen or the desire to speed up work and lower costs is unrecorded.

The rustic character of Fairview's exterior is limited to the use of solid-log construction and peeled logs for beams, posts, and railings. Windows and doors are framed with logs, but all cutting is precise, with none of the decorative elements Durant added by slightly overlapping the trim or extending one piece past the end of another.

Interiors reveal an interesting feature of Fairview's construction, showing the main lodge to be transitional from log-siding-on-wood-framing to solid-log construction. From the outside, the well-matched logs give the building a refined, finished appearance. From the inside, the main lodge's construction is seen as crudely shaped horizontal logs of irregularly matched taper, the wide joints filled with plaster chink-

Camp Fairview's precise log-siding exteriors contrast with the square-cut, roughly-matched, horizontal log framing of the interior. Plaster joint-chinking alternates with the finished log.

ing. In fact, the building is of solid log construction and is sheathed with split logs to give a more elegant look to the structure.

Interiors of Fairview display the combinations Durant introduced at Pine Knot. Interior log surfaces are peeled and varnished. A cement plaster between joints provides a weather seal and a contrast to the log surfaces. Furnishings incorporate rustic furniture of logs, twigs, and peeled bark. Walls were decorated with Japanese fans, screens, and prints; hides and skins were scattered on floors and furniture.

IN 1879, William West Durant's cousin, Frederick, came to the central Adirondacks to follow his relatives' interests in developing the region for tourists. His father had already acquired Osprey Island. Frederick completely abandoned his father's sugar-refining business in New York and devoted his full attention to creating the Prospect House on Blue Mountain Lake in 1880. In the same year he began work on a camp on Forked Lake.

Camp Cedars, second in the early Raquette Lake era, illustrates many Durant-inspired features. It also demonstrates the accretive forms seen in later Great Camps, here the result of almost fifty years of building additions. The original main lodge is of the same design as the earlier main building at Fairview. (In fact, if the main lodges at the three camps could be viewed side by side, they would appear almost identical.) Differing from Fairview with its use of log sheathing, The Cedars is solid-log construction: log corners are notched and project beyond the end of the building, shadows from the log ends becoming decorative features. The transition from using logs as sheathing to using logs as structural elements is completed and the result is a building more rustic and rugged, taking on the appearance of a stockade. Sometime during its development, a small one-story extension was added to the main lodge, resembling Durant's small, bark-covered, log-framed additions at Pine Knot and Uncas. The building wing is framed in vertical, unpeeled logs, with smaller logs three to four inches in diameter used as horizontal and vertical framing pieces. The exterior surface is harmoniously sheathed in cedar bark.

Recorded by three extraordinary photographers over a fifty year period — Seneca Ray Stoddard, Edward Bierstadt, and later, Margaret Bourke-White — The Cedars can be seen as an interpretation of Durant's finest innovations. Also visible are the efforts of camp owners to modify the structures to changing family needs. Minor additions were also required to adjust the buildings to Adirondack weather, such as gutters, downspouts, and passages connecting camp structures.

Photographs taken by Bourke-White in the summer of 1934 reveal the care and precision demanded by Durant's cousin at The Cedars.

Camp Cedars

99

The foundation wall of the main lodge was constructed of solid stone. Logs used for the walls were carefully matched for size and taper, saddle-notched at corners. They were fitted so tightly that the unpeeled exteriors required only hemp caulking as a weather seal. On the interior, the logs were peeled and varnished, and white plaster was used to chink the joints and provide a decorative touch. Where windows and doors are cut into the exterior, unpeeled spruce logs frame the openings. Porch supports, braces, and handrails of peeled spruce poles continue the harmonious treatment.

One feature of The Cedars is uncommon in the Great Camps. As additions to the main lodge were built, they enclosed outdoor space, eventually forming a courtyard. The sense of free-standing buildings remains — the log corners define the volume of each structure — but an intimacy has been created, resembling the compounds of northern Scandinavia and Japan. This enclosing effect evolved over many summers' building campaigns.

The care that went into the exterior construction is reflected in the interiors. For example, the spruce purlins that support the ridge roof are peeled and varnished to match interior walls, but are unpeeled to match the exteriors as they emerge through the walls to support roof overhangs. The relatively short roof span, moreover, obviated cross-

Another Durant cousin, Frederick, created Camp Cedars on Forked Lake. Similar in form to nearby Raquette Lake camps, the main buildings were true log structures. Exterior log surfaces were left unpeeled; interior surfaces were peeled and polished, contrasting with the plaster chinking.

bracing at wall height, creating an interior space completely open to the underside of the roof.

Photographs reveal that furnishings were a mixture of the rustic and Japanese decorations, the fad of the day. On one wall the owner mixed snowshoes, woodblock prints, hides, and fans. A Japanese screen stands next to a bed covered with an American Indian blanket, and Oriental rugs as well as skins to cover the floors.

Not evident in any of the three camps are the stone fireplaces that Durant used as features of both the exterior massing and interior spaces. What they did have were funnel fireplaces in the center of the central social space. (The Cedars provides the best example.) Sheet-metal cones three to four feet in diameter were suspended several feet above the hearth and connected to a pipe extending through the roof. The exacting masonry demanded by Durant and incorporated into his buildings at great cost was to be used by camp owners in other areas of the Adirondacks but not repeated again at Raquette Lake. A more modestly scaled fireplace of rustic stone was built in each of the main lodges at Fairview, The Cedars, and Echo Camp but they are not seen from the exterior.

A severe windstorm in November 1950 destroyed parts of the camp; the early buildings were then removed by the present owner, C. V. Whitney. On its site is a modern camp built in the 1950s. Although the only evidence of The Cedars exists in photographs, many of its characteristic features can be seen in Echo Point Camp, still standing today.

The Wigwam, Camp Cedars, Forked Lake.

THE THIRD of the early Raquette Lake camps was started on the tip of Long Point within five years after William West Durant began building Pine Knot. Echo Camp has been in continual use since it was built by Governor Phineas C. Lounsbury of Connecticut in 1883, and for the past forty years has been maintained as a private girls' camp. The transition from frame construction with log sheathing to the structural use of logs with rustic decoration seen at Fairview and The Cedars is fully achieved in this complex, again fully representative of Durant's influence. All the buildings of the complex have views of the water, but the camp is essentially an enclave in the woods.

Echo Camp's main lodge is identical to those at Fairview and The Cedars: a low, central hall flanked by two-story towers. Several stylistic treatments explored earlier appear as refinements at Echo. The verticality of the main-lodge towers is emphasized by balconies facing the lake. Lacking the visual impact of massive overhanging balconies created at other camps by extension of gables, here they appear as modest attachments to the main buildings. However, the various elements are made harmonious by the introduction of bowed logs in all porches and balconies, creating arched beams. Twigs and branches

Echo Point Camp

emphatically evoke the rustic, spelling out 'ECHO CAMP' in the balcony railing of the main lodge.

Original main lodge and family quarters at Echo were of solid log construction with saddle-notched corners like The Cedars. Exterior materials in the original buildings at Fairview and The Cedars were limited to massive logs and rustic decorative materials; Echo's owners added structural materials and modified the building mass with towers. Closer to Raquette Lake Village than The Cedars, Echo benefited from better access to materials and skilled labor. More time-consuming details were incorporated into the log work. For example, workers

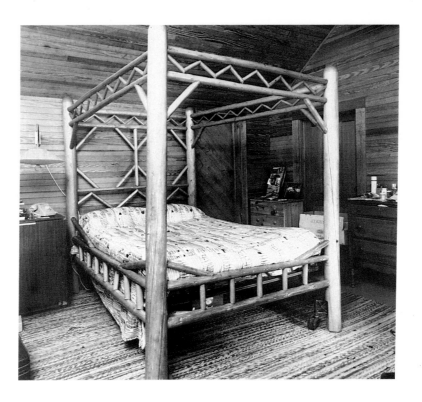

At Echo Camp, a rustic interpretation of a canopied bed.

stepped the logs to support roof overhangs rather than use the simpler technique of diagonal bracing. Logs were fitted precisely; hemp was used for caulking on the exteriors, and interior surfaces were finished with varnished pine planking and narrow wainscoting on walls and some ceilings.

Several of the main-lodge windows vary from the typical vertical-pivoted rectangular windows. Wide, horizontal-fixed windows with a large central pane, surrounded by decorative leaded panels, provide a frame for views of the lake from the main living room. Additional interior light comes from large half-round clerestory windows, a treatment used in the main lodge and for smaller cabins.

Top, *the stockade-like structure at Echo Camp, complex in mass and sensitively scaled, with structure and rustic work providing decoration.* Left, *fan windows in the clerestory of the north and south eaves of guest cabins provided daylight to the interiors.* Right, *original cedar sheathing at Echo Camp shows the wear of forty years of campers' hands.*

Probably the most interesting exterior treatment at Echo is the sheathing of several outbuildings. Spruce bark, peeled and applied as a wall covering, has weathered to a dark brown over time. Frayed at some corners and peeling off framing logs, the fine texture of the material harmonizes with the unpeeled logs of the main lodge.

Along with Pine Knot on Long Point, Echo Camp sustains the finest qualities of the Durant influence on Raquette Lake in the 1880s. Other important Great Camps followed on the lake, the nature and desires of camp owners leading to stylistic differences.

Stott (Collier),
Ten Eyck
(Carnegie),
and
Inman Camps

THREE OTHER important Raquette Lakes camps are the Stott family camp built on Bluff Point in 1877; the Ten Eyck family camp built further up the lake on North Point in 1878; and the Inman family camp built on Round Island in the early 1890s.

Frank Stott of Stottville, New York, came to Raquette Lake to build a camp the same year as Thomas C. Durant. He was a textile manufacturer in New York City and returned to the area for several summers on fishing trips before acquiring the peninsula on the east side of the lake north of Durant. The original Stott camp was a collection of one-story log buildings and pavilions framed in logs.

Unlike Durant's more delicately scaled and detailed buildings, Stott's camp was a complex of solid log structures, resembling log cabins built by early settlers in the Pennsylvania and Delaware area.

Main structures were of square-hewn logs with corners of square-cut dovetails, a treatment uncommon in the Adirondack camps. Although ponderous in construction, the buildings gave an air of classic proportion with evenly spaced, round log columns supporting verandah roofs. The atmosphere of small pavilions in the woods was carried out in a dining structure that sported a wainscoting of saplings and striped canvas used as a protection from the weather. The only exterior ornamentation is saplings forming a herring-bone pattern in the gables of the main lodge. The square-cut logs were exposed on the interiors, with plaster chinking in the joints and dyed burlap used as an interior wainscoting above the logs. Wide-planked floors were covered with Oriental rugs and hides. Decor was the inevitable mixture of trophies with Japanese fans and prints. The camp, set in the forested lake shore, had a distinctly rough ambience.

The camp as it now exists represents the work of Robert Collier, the magazine publisher, who acquired it in the early 1900s. Collier modified the earlier Stott buildings and expanded the camp to over twenty structures. Roofs were raised to increase interior spaces or add second floors to cabins. The pavilionlike atmosphere was changed to a chalet character by adding gable extensions, balconies, and notched log corners.

Interior modifications were part of the change in the camp's character. Walls and ceilings were covered with narrow, beaded wainscoting, finished with a clear gloss varnish. The original simple fireplaces were

An interior at Camp Stott. Opposite, Camp Stott's log cabins and pavilions, around 1885.

replaced by massive ones of cut stone. An elegant two-story brick fire-place similar to those seen in contemporary stick-style domestic build-ings was added to the main lodge. The ordinary camp furniture was re-placed by rustic pieces, some with intricate inlays of twigs.

Collier's flair was also evident in the sleek launches he introduced to the lake; and in 1912, he brought the first airplane to the region, flying it over his camp. Apparently, besting one's neighbors occurred not only in the construction and furnishings of the camps, but in antics on water and in the air.

Collier eventually modified the Stott camp from a collection of log cabins into a Great Camp interconnected with boardwalks, and fin-ished and furnished in a rustic manner. A trophy lodge with adjoining bowling alleys and an elegant boathouse were added. The construction of a gazebo on a small island connected to the camp by a delicate one-hundred-foot-long footbridge was part of the romantic concept con-verting the early Stott cabins — influenced by Durant and executed by the wealth of a Collier — into a Great Camp.

Collier's footbridge to the teahouse island.

The camp on North Point at Raquette Lake is on the site of one of the early camps that existed when Durant started Pine Knot. James Ten Eyck of Albany selected sites with views of the lake to the south and the mountains beyond. The original buildings were similar to the Stott camp, but when Mrs. Lucy Carnegie, widow of Andrew Carnegie's brother Thomas, bought it in 1902, she refashioned it to suit her own taste. Influence of the Swiss chalets of the Bernese Oberland can be vividly seen in the shallow, pitched roofs with broad overhangs at the gable ends and the eaves; in the ribbons of windows; and in the balconies' fret-work railings. The main lodge and supporting structures were built of logs, felled and milled on the site, and finished with square-cut notched corners. The building plans and execution of interior details suggest influences beyond the techniques of local craftsmen, although no record of an architect exists. The main lodge is an H-plan: one wing containing a two-story living room and family quarters; a connecting wing; and a second wing for dining room and kitchen. This was an early example of the multifunctional structure that became evident in later camps designed by William L. Coulter.

North Point on Raquette Lake, an early campsite, was modified by Lucy Carnegie into a complex of buildings in the Swiss chalet style.

Unlike the rustic log buildings of Raquette Lake influenced by Durant, Carnegie's camp at North Point faithfully reproduced the forms, methods, and construction details of the Swiss chalet.

The main living room is elegantly executed with trusses of square-cut logs in the console form of Bernese chalets. The trusses and interior trim of the room are stained dark blue; wall and ceiling surfaces of planks are painted in a contrasting white. A gallery looks down to the massive fireplace and over the space filled with game trophies of the present owners. Although modernizations have occurred over the years, the main lodge and supporting buildings illustrate the evolution of the Great Camps from Durant's single-purpose compound to the large multifunction buildings designed for wealthy sportsmen seeking more elegance.

The third of the early Raquette Lake camps, the Inman camp, is located on Round Island offshore Raquette Lake village. Horace Inman, who came to the area originally as a friend of Benjamin Brandreth, was a paper-box manufacturer from Amsterdam, New York. The camp, existing today in almost its original condition, has recently been deeded to his children by Harry Inman, a noted international lawyer, placing it in the hands of the fifth generation of Inmans.

Swiss chalet trusses of intricate corbelling, set against an off-white wall, form the two-story background for a world-wide collection of trophies at Carnegie's North Point Camp.

The Inman camp at
Raquette Lake. Above,
a delicate rustic honey-
moon cabin, photo-
graphed in 1980, and
opposite, *in 1895, with
attached lean-to.* Right,
a fireplace escutcheon
of bottles in a
chimney, remnants of
demolished building.

Compared to other Raquette Lake camps it is a modest complex. Originally there were thirty-six buildings, but some are no longer standing. In scale, the camp is a one-story affair, similar to the earlier tent platforms. In grouping of buildings, it is informal, in Durant's manner, representing a significant step in the transition from family tents to permanent camp buildings.

Buildings are all of wood-frame construction and sheathed with cedar bark, with the exception of the main lodge, which was sheathed with cork, a personal choice of the owner. Rustic ornamentation and log framing for window and door openings provide a cottage atmosphere. (A fine example of an Adirondack lean-to is attached to the 'Honeymoon' cabin.) The decor has a decided Japanese influence, a favorite of Horace Inman, the original builder. Ornamental ironwork was his hobby, and much of the hardware and the elaborate chandeliers was his handiwork.

The camp was also noted for its casino and dance floor, built out over the water. This structure included four guest bedrooms. More unusual, however, was Inman's vegetable and flower garden located on a large floating platform.

Durant's dreams for Raquette Lake over a century ago never materialized. Except for private holdings secured in the nineteenth century, Raquette Lake is owned by the state of New York. Golden Beach on South Bay, the site of an early hotel, now provides hundreds of public campsites, descendents of Durant's vision of bustling villages, streams of tourists, and lake shores lined with cottages.

CHAPTER 7

ST. REGIS LAKE AREA

Tent platforms at the Hooker camp on Upper St. Regis Lake

A T THE SAME TIME that Durant and the early Raquette Lake visitors were building their first camps, families were arriving in the St. Regis lakes area as guests of Paul Smith. An unusual story has been told of this unique setting in a charming little volume called *Camp Chronicles* written by Mrs. Mildred Phelps Stokes Hooker in 1952. Mrs. Hooker spent her first Adirondack summer at a camp on Upper St. Regis Lake at the age of two. She recalls that her father first brought the Stokes family to Paul Smith's hotel in 1875. Like other families seeking their own campsites, the Stokeses went into a rough camp on an island, sleeping on balsam branches and bathing in the lake.

The concentration of guest camps on the shores of Upper St. Regis, Lower St. Regis, Spitfire, and Osgood lakes attested that the area had become quite fashionable towards the turn of the century. By 1896, land in this remote region of the Adirondacks was selling for four thousand dollars an acre, and almost every available parcel was owned and occupied by members of some of America's most prominent families.

The development of the St. Regis area could not be explained in terms of natural beauty. Unlike Raquette Lake and other areas of the Adirondacks abounding with the natural attractions of rugged mountains, mirror-surfaced lakes, or marvelous river chasms, it was the fabled Paul Smith's that attracted early visitors to the St. Regis area. Some of the more adventurous guests, in order to escape the hotel routine, would row out to their favorite spots on the opposite shore and on the island to picnic, returning to the hotel for the evening. The attachment to these day camps grew so quickly that families like the Stokeses decided to buy land, most of which was owned by Smith.

Donaldson quotes Smith's obituary of 1912: 'When he went to the Adirondacks many years ago the woods were full of Indians; when he died they were full of millionaires.' Smith's story belongs to American folklore. Dr. E. L. Trudeau was Smith's guest in his first convalescence in the Adirondacks in 1873, an experience that eventually led to the founding of the famous Trudeau Sanatorium on nearby Saranac Lake. Smith's guests included the leading families of New York, Philadelphia, Baltimore, and Washington; they took cottages for the season and grew so attached to the land and climate that they were pleased to pay the high prices, of purchase or lease, for land on one of the lakes.

The development of Stokes's original camp is typical of other camps in the St. Regis Lake area. Originally the family slept in tents with wooden floors; the same tented scheme was used for the dining room and the living area. There were also several wooden storage buildings and a wood-frame kitchen building. In 1883, log buildings with shingle roofs and painted ends were built. Mrs. Stokes served as the architect

From Canvas to Cabins

Wildair, the earliest of the permanent St. Regis camps, barely intrudes on its setting. Above, *the main lodge, a masterfully executed assemblage of forms and materials, merges with its site.* Right, *details of the main lodge's precisely-cut log sheathing, designed by McKim, Mead and White.* Far right, *Edward Larabee Barnes's 1969 renovations enhanced the interiors with clerestory windows. New finishes match the delicate wainscot and trim details of earlier craftsmen.*

for this early work. In 1884, a breakwater, a summer house, and a main cabin were constructed. After this, Mr. Stokes designed a small Greek temple of logs and wood, which he used as a study. One by one, the tents were replaced by cabins, and later bathrooms were added.

Only a few 'artistic' camps in the Durant style were built in the St. Regis area. Except for Marjorie Merriweather Post's Topridge, created in the 1920s, the camps were not as imposing as those built elsewhere on the Saranac lakes or on private preserves. However, the St. Regis camps generally were not meant to become Great Camps. Excellently crafted, solidly built, and exemplifying forest adaptation, they evolved, despite certain dissimilarities of architectural style, into a homogeneous summer community of remarkable longevity.

Adirondack lawn chairs at Wildair, ruggedly uncomfortable, with the St. Regis Mountains in the distance, beyond Upper St. Regis Lake.

WHITELAW REID, publisher of the New York *Herald-Tribune* and a major public figure of his period, began the earliest 'artistic' camp on Upper St. Regis Lake in 1882. The original buildings were designed by a niece of Reid. Donaldson reports that 'the lady herself made the designs and it was called "Camp Wild Air." It embodied features of rustic beauty and modern comfort which were entirely novel at the time,

Camp Wild Air

and it became in a general way the suggestive model for the similar camps that soon sprang up around it.' Mrs. Hooker recalls her mother commenting after a visit to the new cabin in September 1885, 'Very pretty, just suited for a young lady.' In *Camp Chronicles* Mrs. Hooker adds parenthetically, 'like so many others, she seems to have built before [she] owned.' Several later buildings were designed by New York architects McKim, Mead and White after a fire destroyed the main lodge in 1917. In 1969, Edward Larabee Barnes designed renovations for the main lodge and additional new structures.

The original camp was placed on a relatively flat but heavily wooded site. With characteristic rustic features, each of the buildings had a separate function expressed in an elegant but restrained style unique to the area. It was not long before it was widely imitated. Camp Wild Air focuses on the main lodge, a one-story shingle structure with a unique cruciform-plan living room surmounted by a wooden vaulted ceiling. The soaring space created a distinctly ecclesiastical atmosphere. The Barnes renovations in 1969 included the addition of a kitchen; new clerestory windows and a skylight at the lodge's peak subtly warm the rooms by providing natural light on the yellow-red-tinted, gumwood-paneled walls. Excellently proportioned framing and interior details provide a restful atmosphere.

The main lodge of unpeeled cedar logs, with its wide porches resting on a stone base, dominates the site. McKim, Mead and White take full advantage of the lakeside locations: the sitting and billiard room and Bishop's palace of logs all appear to be floating on the water's surface. Other buildings include an eight-bedroom guest house, workshop-staff house, recreation hall, and a new two-bedroom 'winter house.' Barnes elegant new buildings, with naturally weathered boards and sensitive integration of patios, walks, and steps, complement this Great Camp.

Katia

ONE OF THE attractive features of the St. Regis camps is the modesty of their scale and proportion, and the restrained use of exterior materials. Unpretentious one-story structures, tastefully juxtaposed, are clad in shingles or slab siding. Delicate traceries of diamond-paned windows offer just a hint of the elegant interiors. An excellent example of the unpretentiously-scaled, multibuilding camp is Camp Katia.

Approaching the camp by water through fog early on a summer morning, one is startled by the dramatic boulder-walled boathouse of two interlocking, upright cylinders, forty to fifty feet in diameter, capped by conical roofs. The lakefront volume has a grotto-like appearance, with three arched boat entrances; the rear volume is a two-story playhouse and storage area.

George E. Earle of Philadelphia built the first camp buildings between 1890 and 1894. The family had built several other camps in the Adirondacks — two on Upper Saranac Lake, one at Long Lake and two on Spitfire Lake — before settling on Upper St. Regis. Most of the present fifteen buildings, some of wood and some of stone, were built between 1894 and 1911. Each demonstrates a sophistication in the use of materials unsurpassed in the area at the turn of the century. All of the carefully sited small-scale buildings are interconnected by a wooden boardwalk, which weaves its way through this somewhat swampy site.

Common to the St. Regis lakes area, the buildings are single-function structures, each just large enough to accommodate its purpose. The main cabin, writing house, dining room, and living room are similar in style and materials: wood-framed and shingled, with steeply pitched and shingled roofs. Windows all have large central panes surrounded by a decorative motif of small diamond-shaped leaded panes. Reminiscent of the original tent platforms, seven individual sleeping cabins are set in a row on the edge of the dense woods, connected by a stepped boardwalk.

The main cabin is easily identified from the lake by the camp's name, 'KATIA,' set in a porch gable. The high-ceilinged one-story room, capped by a hip roof and surrounded by lower porches, gives the structure its classic grace and elegance. In comparison to Durant's decorative structures of log work and twigs at Pine Knot, this building is elegantly composed. The exterior sheathing of small shingles, the repetitive window openings, the equally spaced porch columns and pervasive symmetry, reinforce its classic simplicity.

The interior space is a delight of light-colored horizontal boards that cover the walls and extend upward as the ceiling. The diamond-shaped panes that frame the main windows are repeated in the clerestory windows, creating a balance of natural daylight. This clever device creates a rhythm and sensitive composition seen elsewhere on the St. Regis lakes but seldom in other parts of the Adirondacks. The result is a space of shimmering light unlike the dark spaces typical of Adirondack camps.

INEVITABLY, there are Great Camp complexes that defy categorization but cannot be ignored. Although a camp may have all the features of a private family retreat in the rustic style and be a compound of self-sufficient structures, and thus seem at first glance to qualify as a Great Camp, an owner's fancy in the selection of construction material and detail makes its identity doubtful as such. Two camps on the St. Regis lakes illustrate this point.

Cobblestones and Pagodas

119

In the summer morning's early light, Katia's grotto-like boathouse is reflected in the still waters of Upper St. Regis Lake. Above, *two interlocking drums, built of cobblestones taken from the lake's shore, support the distinctive conical roofs.* Right, *delicate diamond-shaped panes form the typical Katia cabin window, set in shingled walls. The scale of the camp's structures is small, and the use of exterior materials and trim is restrained.*

120

Broad eaves and a wide porch surround the modest-sized 'Living Room.' Diamond-shaped window surrounds are repeated in the clerestory windows above. Above, typical of the refined St. Regis camps, Katia is different from Durant's work, but elegantly rustic nonetheless. Left, at Camp Katia, tent platforms have been enclosed to make permanent guest cabins.

A unique expression of vernacular camp architecture, Camp Cobblestone reflects the owner's personal taste.

Camp Cobblestone's unique feature is indicated by the camp's name. Located on Spitfire Lake just across the ridge from Katia on Upper St. Regis, it is similar to Katia in form, maintaining the same low scale, octagonal and round building volumes, diamond-paned windows, and clerestories. The similarities, however, are more than coincidental, for George H. Earle, Jr., the owner of Katia, built Cobblestone for his daughters.

The obvious difference between the camps is in the selection of local cobblestone for the exteriors at Cobblestone, whereas at Katia only the boathouse exhibits this feature. The former consists of an octagonal living cabin; a dining and kitchen cabin; a boathouse and tower; a round bedroom cabin built out over the water; two guest cabins; and service buildings. In addition, there were several large wooden cabins of four to six bedrooms each on a higher ridge near the forest. The propitiousness of building the main cabins of stone was demonstrated when the sleeping cabins were partially destroyed by fire in 1966.

The only camp on the St. Regis lakes built of these stones, it probably reflected the particular interest of the original owner. The camp is
readily recognized from the lake by its boathouse and adjoining two-
story tower. The stone living room is similar in octagonal plan to its
wood-frame counterpart at Katia. Even with large single windows of
diamond panes set in the stone walls, the scale of the building is imposing, for it is not tempered by surrounding porches. Additional
openings for natural lighting are provided by 'eyebrow-shaped' dormers typical of the period's shingle-style buildings. Interior spaces,
open to the rafters, reveal the intricate framing required to form
arched dormers into hip roofs. The interior is finished in either fir or
western pine with several massive cobblestone fireplaces.

As startling as the stone towers of Cobblestone may appear, they
are easily outdone by the pagodas of Pine Tree Point. This early camp
on Upper St. Regis Lake was originally built by H. M. Twombly as a
collection of small buildings with exteriors of vertical board and bat-
tens. Just back from a trip to Japan, the Frederick Vanderbilt family

*'Eyebrow' dormers
match the carpenter's
art with that of Cobble-
stone's masons.*

123

Pine Tree Point's pagoda on Upper St. Regis Lake.

Above, *Pine Tree Point's boat dock and main lodge, rebuilt by Frederick Vanderbilt in the traditional* Irimoya *roof form of Japanese temples*. Left, *the main boathouse at Pine Tree Point is a Victorian structure, repainted seasonally in its original pale blues and greens.*

purchased the camp in 1902 and set about reconstructing it in its present style. Thinking the lake very Japanese (Whiteface Mountain even reminded them of Fujiyama), they hired the Japanese workmen who had completed the Japanese Village at the Buffalo, New York, World's Fair to recreate the Japanese country homes they had admired in their travels. In her *Camp Chronicles,* Mrs. Hooker states that 'They not only had the cabins Japanized, they dressed all their maids in kimonos! They had taken over a stout English maid of Mother's and she nearly died of embarrassment when she had to appear before us in this new uniform.' Camp Pine Tree Point consists of one semicircular main cabin with a delicately pitched roof; sleeping cabin attached to the main cabin by boardwalks; a decorative summer house in the style of a small pagoda; several small guest cottages; and a small landing and larger boathouse. The Vanderbilts sought a highly refined re-creation of the Japanese models in both interiors and exteriors, but the limitations of materials and the fact that the job was a reconstruction, rather than wholly original work, allowed only partial success.

Longwood

OF THE MANY camps on the shores of the St. Regis lakes, probably the only complex with all the characteristics of an Adirondack Great Camp is Longwood, built and still owned by the Brewster family. George S. Brewster originally came to Saranac Lake in 1904 to recover from tuberculosis. In 1906 he purchased the campsite on Spitfire Lake, completing the typical Great Camp complex over a two-year building campaign.

The well-organized grouping of buildings on the site and the continuity of design and craftsmanship in construction can be attributed to the owner's taste, the architect's talent, and the contractor's skill. Brewster chose the New York architect Robert F. Stephenson to design and supervise construction of the camp. Ben Muncil, Jr., a local contractor, more widely known for his work at the Post camp at Topridge, was the builder who interpreted the rustic details.

Although the camp didn't evolve from tent platforms, separate cabins were constructed, as was then fashionable. The site, accessible only by water, compactly contains family quarters and service buildings. Living cabin, dining cabin, and kitchen complex are oriented to the water, with the owner's and guests' cabins strung out behind these central buildings. Several boathouses stretch along the lakefront, and service buildings are scattered throughout the site.

The strongest impression the camp gives is of the harmony of the buildings and the setting. As with Durant's camp Pine Knot, selection and placement of structural materials tie the different building forms together. Unpeeled log posts provide the framing. Beams, rafters

At Camp Longwood, exposed, peeled, and polished log studs, rafters, and purlins, with plank walls and ceiling.

studding, and sills are of hemlock, while rafters are constructed of peeled spruce or cedar, and the roof is shingled in cedar. Features typifying the style include unpeeled cedar logs — flattened on top and bottom — for lower walls up to the window sills, and cedar bark nailed to wood sheathing from sills to the roof plates. Log joists of spruce extend to support overhanging eaves, reinforced by diagonal braces of unpeeled cedar posts. Rows of windows rest on the lower wall of logs. Structural framing, by either courses of logs or post-and-beam, is dominant. This treatment, combined with the other surfaces composed of in-filling of bark sheathing, windows, or open spaces, evokes the character of Japanese country houses.

Interior spaces in the main structures open up to expose the structural framing of the roof. Clerestory windows are introduced in side walls and gable ends, bringing light to interiors shadowed by extensive overhangs. In the main cabin, the lower band of logs is exposed on the interior as peeled and polished surfaces. Exterior joints are caulked with oakum and filled with moss on the inside. Post-and-beam framing moves from floor to roof plate with logs graded in size so that major supports are larger than the vertical or horizontal logs that function only as studding. Floors and wall sheathing are pine planking.

The shallow, sloping roofs, repeated in main and service buildings, boathouses, and walkways, add gracefulness to the complex. Shaggy cedar sills are topped by sheathing of silvery gray cedar bark and

127

post-and-beam framing of bark-covered logs. Railings, structural braces, and door and window frames continue the harmonious treatment, also using unpeeled logs. Monotony of the wood tones is avoided by modest touches of color and decoration. Planters and pots filled with geraniums on porches and covered walkways counterpoint the woody grays and browns. An unbroken link to the decorative fashions of the turn of the century is discerned in the Japanese paper lanterns that are suspended along exterior walkways and hang inside from rafters.

Longwood represents the happy combination of an architect sensitive to local style, and a remarkable builder, merging their talents to achieve a harmonious effect. The architect designed the basic building forms, selected placement of window and door openings, and matched the owner's needs with careful planning of interior and intrabuilding spaces. But the specifications and drawings had to be interpreted with local materials and the skills of the builder. Muncil's selection of logs, for walls, for columns or for window frames, was an artist's judgment. The 'right' log had to have proper length, taper, and diameter to be structurally sound and match the adjacent log or pole in color and surface texture. Skilled hands flattened each log, from coped column to beam, taking care never to 'bruise' a log or remove its bark. Though Durant's experimentation in derivative forms and decoration was avoided, at Longwood, local craftsmen and the architect were able to create a camp perfectly suited to its woodland setting.

Longwood's silver-gray exteriors blend into the wooded setting. Opposite above and left, the cabin framing of Longwood's lower walls is of unpeeled notched logs, planed at top and bottom. The upper walls are sheathed with peeled spruce bark. The exterior of the two-story main cabin is compatible with that of the one-story buildings. Outdoor decks, reached through grouped French doors, are an extension of the interior space. Opposite right and below, Longwood's boat shelter 'floats' its roof on log columns.

129

CHAPTER 8

SARANAC LAKES AREA

Stillman's 'Philosophers Camp'

THE INTERNATIONAL reputation of Saranac Lake is synonymous with Dr. Edward Livingston Trudeau and his sanatorium for tuberculosis patients. Trudeau came to the Adirondacks in 1873 to die, but miraculously recovered, and lived to found his famous sanatorium at Saranac Lake Village in 1884.

But in the 1820s, long before Trudeau came to the area, a settlement had developed at the east end of Lower Saranac Lake. One Jacob Smith Moody came to what is now the village of Saranac Lake in 1819 and had no neighbors for ten miles in any direction. Three years later Captain Pliny Miller settled nearby and in the 1840s built a small hotel, the first in the region. William Martin came to the village in 1849, leased Miller's hotel and later built his own. Following Martin, Virgil Bartlett arrived, leased Miller's hotel and soon built a hotel for himself on the carry between Middle and Upper Saranac lakes.

By the mid-1850s the area was the headquarters for lumbermen and tourists. Readily available guides, boats, and camping supplies were secured from the hotels. Hammond, Agassiz, and Headley started their travels at Martin's; Lady Murray and the Reverend Murray were guests there as well; Colvin, Ely, Wallace, and Stoddard all recorded their visits here. Both the Reverend Murray and Wallace gave the hotel a 'four-star' rating, Murray describing it as 'the most convenient point at which to meet your guides.' The host was 'good natured and gentlemanly' and 'the celebrated Long Lake guides and their unrivalled boats' headquartered there. Wallace, in his 1875 *Guide* found it a jumping-off place for 'parties, including a goodly sprinkling of women' for excursions to nearby lakes.

Among the early campers were the members of the 'Philosophers Camp,' led by William Stillman. The group of ten distinguished Cambridge intellectuals included Ralph Waldo Emerson, James Russell Lowell, and Louis Agassiz. Longfellow had been invited but declined to come when he heard Emerson was bringing a gun. The group established a camp west of the Saranacs on Follensby Pond in 1858. In 1859 they founded the 'Adirondack Club,' purchased land on Ampersand Pond south of the Saranacs and built 'Camp Maple.' However, the Civil War intervened, and the club was neglected and forgotten.

The Follensby Pond camp was recorded by Stillman in a painting, and by Emerson in a poem. Stillman's painting of a group of gallused campers among giant pines three to four feet in diameter captures the wilderness character admirably. Emerson stands isolated in the center of the painting, Agassiz behind the stump to the left with John Holmes, Dr. Estes Howe, and Dr. Jeffries Wyman. To Emerson's right are E. R. Hoar, James Russell Lowell, and the artist himself. Horatio Woodman is about to fire his rifle at the target intently watched by four guides.

Philosophers, Hotels, and a Doctor

131

Emerson described the beauties of the Adirondacks in sufficiently glowing terms to fuel the imagination of future visitors.

> Next morn, we swept with oars the Saranac with skies of benediction, to Round (Middle Saranac) Lake, where all the sacred mountains drew around us, Tahawus, Seward, MacIntyre, Baldhead, and other titans without muse or name. Pleased with these grand companies, we glide on, instead of flowers, crowned with a wreath of hills.

Emerson portrays the lakes and shallows edged with banks of flowers and lilies, unbroken forests, and deer feeding at water's edge, all scenes to entice the city dweller north to the woods. It was a place innocent of civilization where one found

> No placard on these rocks warned to the polls,
> No door-bell heralded a visitor,
> No corner waits, no letter came or went,
> Nothing was ploughed, or reaped, or bought, or sold;
> The frost might glitter, it would blight no crop,
> The falling rain will spoil no holiday.

With the early hotels proving popular and Murray proclaiming the area's hospitality, new lodges and hotels opened to welcome fresh waves of travelers. Like the Philosophers, other visitors became interested in building their own camps on the lakes. Visitors to Saranac Inn, opened at the north end of Upper Saranac in 1864, started to ferret out their own sites for day camping. Soon, tent platforms were built and, as at Paul Smith's, shorefront land was purchased for camps.

A guest lodge, built in 1878 on Upper Saranac Lake's southwest shore, was connected by road to Tupper Lake. The lodge was replaced in 1891 by the elegant Wawbeek Inn. (A sad footnote — the Inn, rebuilt after a fire in 1915, was completely burned out in 1980.) From the Wawbeek, a steamboat line was established to the Saranac Inn. Eventually, this line provided access to camps on the shores of Upper Saranac, delivering mail, groceries, hardware, and other supplies. The construction of a railroad spur in 1875 made the area more accessible, and by 1880 private camps began to be built on the lake's northwest shore.

Two events of the 1880s choked off rapid development of Saranac camps. In 1882 the Adirondack Railway Company bought almost 12,000 acres of land bordering the Upper Saranac, intending it for use in extending the railroad and for future land sales. Additional acquisitions by William West Durant brought the Railway holdings to almost 20,000 acres. At the same time, New York State's formation of the

Forest Preserve in 1885 excluded much of the state-owned land around the lakes from any form of commercial activity or private residential camp buildings.

The twofold action of railroad speculation and state policy limited development of Great Camps on Upper Saranac to privately owned land. When the extension of the projected railroad did not materialize, Durant sold his holdings to several individuals in 1890. Acquisition for speculation was repeated around the Saranac Inn in 1886 when new purchasers bought the surrounding township of almost 27,000 acres, including most of the land at the northern end of the lake.

While St. Regis, Raquette, and other accessible lakes in the central Adirondacks became dotted with Great Camps, the Saranacs saw relatively little development. The region's largest connected lakes remained protected, kept in the condition observed by William Stillman:

> Ampersand Pond was certainly the most beautiful site I have ever seen in Adirondack Country. Virgin forest save where trappers or hunters had cut wood for their camp-fires, the tall pines standing in their ranks along the shores of a little lake that lay in the middle of the estate, encircled by mountains . . . clothed to their summits in primeval woods. In a little valley where a crystal spring sent its water down to the lake, and a grove of deciduous trees gave high and airy shelter, I pitched a camp.

From Adventures in the Wilderness: *'O, royal sight it was to see them come one after another over the verge.'*

Upper Saranac Lake

One alternative to a shorefront site for a camp was a large tract of land containing attractive lakes and ponds for incorporation into a private club or preserve. As the Adirondacks' appeal spread more widely among the Eastern establishment, creators of new fortunes sought land for campsites from earlier holdings, from lumbermen sometimes owning whole towns, or from speculators like Paul Smith or Durant. And herein is a distasteful feature of American culture in the last quarter of the nineteenth century, one affecting the development of Great Camps in the Saranac Lake area.

Among the assemblers of wealth in this period were families like Seligman, Loeb, Schiff, Guggenheim, Bache, and Kahn. They were Jews and, although tolerated as financiers of industrial expansion, they were not readily welcomed in resorts established by gentiles. Occasionally a Schiff or a Warburg could buy a major holding on the Maine coast or Jersey Shore, but those who held Adirondack land were hardly as welcoming. An incident of discrimination at Saratoga's Grand Union Hotel in 1877 against the influential Joseph Seligman and his family fueled a national debate over anti-Semitism. The Grand Union's policy gave other hotels and clubs a precedent, and anti-Semitism in Adirondack resorts became more blatant, with hotels boldly advertising 'Hebrews need not apply,' and 'Hebrews will knock vainly for admission.' Among the unsavory records of this attitude is the blatant discriminatory practice of the Lake Placid Club, which published a code declaring it impracticable to make Jews welcome. Hotels, lake owners' associations, or clubs could and did dictate their own rules, and they exercised a strict control over who could become guests, members, or purchasers of adjacent lands. The term 'restricted' soon became part of the Adirondack lexicon.

When Durant sold off his land around Upper Saranac Lake in the early 1890s, some Jewish millionaires responded. The builders of the Adirondack railroad were more interested in the ready cash than in the proper parentage of potential buyers, and were willing to make their

View from the boat-house at the Knoll-wood Club, Lower Saranac Lake.

**The Grand
Lodge Emerges**

land available to anyone able to pay the asking price. The wealthy Jewish financiers began purchasing sites along the lake. They built near friends, creating camps for their large families in an area that had seen little previous camp development. Non-Jews as well continued the Adirondack land rush between 1895 and 1910, and Great Camps of imposing proportions were built. Several of the camps were designed by architects who practiced in Saranac Lake Village: William Coulter, later Coulter and Westhoff; and the successor firm, William Distin. Coulter was an admirer of Durant, and his designs followed Durant's influence, sometimes incorporating owners' particular preferences for what they remembered from their childhoods in southern Germany, and other times relying upon the Queen Anne or shingle style as sources. The number of camp buildings and the scale of the main cabins were substantial, often multistory structures grander and more elegant than anything on the Raquette or St. Regis lakes.

The Saranac area camps are presented in this chapter chronologically. One was built on Lower Saranac Lake, the remainder on Upper Saranac, all between 1895 and 1930. Although other Great Camps were built on the lakes, these have been either destroyed or radically altered. As a group, the Saranac Lake camps represent the transition from the tent platform pattern to the Adirondack-style grand lodges. Coulter, Distin, and their successors transformed Durant's small-scale buildings into massive Adirondack hunting lodges executed with becoming sensitivity and taste. In contrast to the unpretentious deer-hunting camps near the Saranac Inn, favored by former President Cleveland in the early 1900s, the camps of Morton, Kahn, Lewisohn, Bache, Seligman, Loeb, and Rockefeller were luxurious; they were indeed playgrounds of the rich.

**Pinebrook
and Moss
Ledge**

AN EARLY Saranac Lake camp builder was Levi P. Morton, a former Vice President of the United States and governor of New York. Morton, purchasing Eagle Island and adjacent mainland property in 1898, hired William Coulter to design a modest rustic lodge for the island and other buildings on the lakeshore. The camp was described in Martin B. Ives' book *Through the Adirondack in Eighteen Days* (1899):

> A trip around the lake is one much to be enjoyed, for its shores are thickly ornamented and beautified by numerous private camps, at the docks of which the steamer stops on signal, and some of which are expensive and novel examples of rustic architecture. One of these is the camp or cottage of that 'grand old man' and much admired and esteemed friend, ex-governor Levi P. Morton.

The mainland camp was called 'Pinebrook,' named after a small brook bounded by pine saplings on the property. Nine buildings were raised in the camp's first year: two guest cabins, staff quarters for butler, maids, cook, waitress and gardener, a dining building, a boathouse, and a launch house. A plank walk extended from the dock offshore to a small covered tea house.

In an arrangement similar to tent-platform camps, individual sleeping cabins were connected by boardwalks and covered walkways to the central building. Coulter's main lodge made decorative use of a log screen filling the high, open-gabled ends, keeping the interior cool during the day. The gable screening was repeated on smaller cabins and integrated into the roof framing of the covered walkways. This same screen device was later used elsewhere by Coulter, who became more adventurous in the size of the logs and degree of decoration. The proportions of the main lodge incorporated elements of the Swiss chalet traditions: a broad, shallow, sloping roof with wide protective overhangs, and a balcony rail of scroll-cut boards. Fires and subsequent later reconstruction have altered the exterior of the Morton camp, but its multibuilding character remains.

While Governor Morton was building Pinebrook, the property to the northeast was being developed by Miss Isabel Ballantine of New York. The camp was called 'Moss Ledge,' a name suggested by a rocky, moss-covered ledge still to be seen jutting into the lake. Although it is unknown if Coulter designed the buildings at Moss Ledge, they display the character and log detailings of Pinebrook. A main lodge was built first, followed by a guest cabin, dining building, boathouse, garage, and launch house. On a promontory of land a distance from the main camp, a tea house was built overlooking the lake. At its zenith as a private camp, Moss Ledge was staffed by a cook, chambermaid, chaffeur-boatman, and gardener.

Unpeeled logs for structural framing were used in both camps, some buildings of notched-log construction and others with plank wall-sheathing and shingles over log frames. Log joinery and construction detail for cabin framing, railings, and walkways are finely executed.

Morton sold Pinebrook to Mitchell Levy in 1903. Unfortunately, much of the camp was destroyed in a fire in 1911. It was rebuilt by a new owner in 1915, who rebuilt in the same Swiss chalet style, using rustic details. The camp was owned for a brief period by a Laughlin of the steel family, then purchased by Carl Loeb, a New York investment banker, in 1933. The Loebs gave the camp to Syracuse University in 1948, purchasing Moss Ledge and including it in the gift. After many years of use as a conference center, it was sold in the early 1970s and today is again a private camp.

Camp Pinebrook. Opposite top, *a quartercentury after Durant, the Swiss chalet motif was simplified and relieved of any rustic touches. Details at Moss Ledge:* opposite below, *the decorative porch railing required precise coping to fit every piece in place;* above, *a gable fan provides structural support for a roof extended over a porch;* left, *camp cabins, connected by a cascade of porch roofs.*

Knollwood Club

ON A ROAD along the northeast shore of Lower Saranac Lake, about two miles from Saranac Lake Village, a driver's eye may be caught by an unpretentious rustic camp entrance. The camp's name, 'KNOLL-WOOD,' spelled out in twigs and framed by logs supported by stone pillars, provides a gateway to one of the most carefully planned and executed of the Great Camps.

At about the same time that William Coulter was designing Governor Morton's Pinebrook and Vanderbilt's Sagamore, he took on a commission from a group of six friends and their families. Having previously summered at the Childwold Hotel, the friends decided to purchase land and form their own club. Acquiring five hundred acres of land, they hired Coulter to design a complex, and the Saranac firm of Branch and Callanan to do the building. The original families were those of Louis Marshall, Daniel Guggenheim, Elias Ashiel, George Blumenthal, Abram N. Stein, and Max Nathan. The camp remains today in the hands of the children and families of the original owners.

The site is heavily wooded, sloping down to the shore. With the exception of a few small service buildings scattered along the entrance road, the main camp buildings all face the lake.

In developing the commission in 1899, the architects created a collection of rustic structures affording individual privacy for each family while retaining a sense of community. This was achieved by providing houses for the individual families to serve as sleeping units, and a central 'casino' to act as dining and recreation building. The pattern is similar to older clubs in the Adirondacks but was rarely carried through with such fine continuity of design, site features, and building orientation. As a result of a brisk and remarkably efficient building campaign, the main buildings were completed in one year, the families using the camp for the first time in the summer of 1900.

Coulter set about designing six identical two-and-a-half story Victorian shingle homes, the casino, and a boathouse. His adroit talents created a rustic masterpiece of sensitively sited and unpretentious buildings, with extraordinarily imaginative rustic work throughout. The family cottages, while oriented to the lake, are barely visible through a lakefront screen of trees. A wooden boardwalk on the uphill side of the cottages threads through the forest linking the buildings together. Bridges of different rustic design span from the boardwalk into the midlevel entrance of each cottage.

In plan, the cottages contained living rooms, a small service kitchen, and four to six bedrooms. The working drawings numbered the family units one through six and lots were drawn to determine ownership. Isolated by the camera or viewed side by side, this collection of excellently preserved camp buildings represents a high point of Great Camp rustic architecture. Two-and-a-half story log porches wrap the

The rustic entrance gate at the Knollwood Club.

three sides of the cottages facing the lake. Soaring log gables, tier upon tier, in fans, sunburst panels, and geometric patterns on the six side-by-side buildings are in themselves thrilling. In a tour-de-force of imaginative design, the architects transformed what were essentially period, shingle-frame houses into six unique rustic cottages. Peeled logs used in the decorative triangular screen marked the attic level directly below the roof line. Dark shadows created by the deeply set porches, especially by the wooden screens, give to each camp an oddly light and skeletal appearance — as if nothing but the framework existed and the interior were a hollow space.

The original interiors of the six cottages were almost identical. The lower floors contained a large living area with several smaller spaces off to the sides, a small service kitchen and pantry, and in some, a bedroom. A massive granite fireplace dominated the center of each cottage living room. The ceilings were low, supported on rough-hewn beams that sometimes retained the original bark. These rooms were

An ornately furnished living room at Knollwood, with diamond-shaped shingles between adze-hewn columns and beams.

Above, *Knollwood's six modest two-and-one-half story frame cottages were connected by wooden boardwalks and timber bridge. Opposite, Knollwood Club cottages, each with unique screen. Tapering columns rise from the first-floor porch to the roof. The composition is 'gridded' by horizontals marking the floors, and the diagonal bracing is reflected in the railings and gable fans. The six cottages and other major Club buildings form a tour-de-force of rustic architecture. Right, Knollwood boathouse with second-floor recreation room.*

filled with Indian craft objects, fishing gear, japonoiserie, and a combination of Mission style–Stickley and Glasgow School wooden furniture.

The casino, used till the 1930s as the central dining room and social center of the Knollwood Club, is a two-story polygonal structure with a hipped rather than gabled roof. Set back from the shore, it stands behind the two-story main boathouse. Families gathered for meals in the first-floor dining room, the second floor providing recreational space. As in the main camps, porches wrap the exterior and peeled logs are used for railings and structural framing. Massive stone fireplaces were set at either end of the large, open interior spaces on each floor.

The focal point of daily activity, today as from the club's inception, is the boathouse. The rectangular, two-story building is log framed with an overhanging verandah extending entirely around the building on the second floor. The first level of the boathouse contains boat slips, the second floor an open space used as a game room. Long walkways extend from the boathouse along the shoreline, turn out onto the lake, and terminate in two octagonal pergolas.

When the club was first designed, Knollwood's members believed that the setting for their camp and the natural state of the site was as important as the structures they intended to build. Unfortunately, little remains of the original shorefront landscaping, carried out in the Japanese manner. Gone are the narrow footbridges across several tiny islands connected to the shore. Gone, too, is a small writing pavilion on the lake. But the spirit of the club founders, who believed that the summer at Knollwood should be a family experience shared with friends in a pleasant woodland setting, is retained. Now on a summer's day, the baskets of geraniums, the planters filled with flowers, and continuing waterfront activities accent Knollwood's vitality. Planned and built more than eighty years ago, Knollwood is enjoyed by a fourth generation of users.

Otto Kahn's Camp

THE VERSATILITY of the Saranac Lake architects — and their ability to satisfy clients' desires — is shown in the camp William Coulter designed for Otto Kahn, the New York financier. Built on Bull Point on Upper Saranac Lake, just north of the Wawbeek Inn, the project started at about the same time Coulter was designing the rustic Knollwood Club and Morton's Eagle Island camp.

Rather than start with the Swiss chalet model, the architect patterned his design after the popular interpretation of English Tudor country houses, made fashionable by the English architect Norman Shaw. Houses of similar style were being designed as vacation homes in the 1880s and 90s by distinguished American architects for Mount

Above, *Otto Kahn's Upper Saranac Lake camp was an unusual combination of Tudor forms and details combined with rustic touches. Left, at Kahn's camp, the lower floors, porches, walkways, and railings were of unpeeled logs, precisely cut and fitted. Architect Coulter satisfied the owner's desire for a pretentious country estate but introduced rustic detail to place the buildings properly in their setting.*

Desert, Maine, Newport, Rhode Island, and the Jersey Shore. Coulter added an appropriate Adirondack touch by mixing timber porches and lower-floor framing with a very proper Tudor upper floor. Building forms — with half-timbered walls, projecting gables, and brick chimneys — transferred the Long Island and Westchester country home to an Adirondack foundation. Long, covered walkways of log construction connected buildings, and other site details were executed in the rustic style.

The Kahn camp is important, not for its combination of styles, but because it represented the earliest of the large country homes built in the Adirondacks. Elsewhere, large log cabins had been built at Santanoni and at Sagamore, but they were compact buildings of low scale with the domestic character of Swiss chalets. With this camp, Coulter began to develop a model that would be expanded on Upper Saranac Lake and other preserves to become the typical Adirondack family lodge. Moderate in size compared to later Saranac Lake Great Camps, Otto Kahn's camp consisted of a main building of three stories, containing living, dining, sleeping, and kitchen space; several large guest houses with bedrooms and sitting rooms in each; a large boathouse and playhouse; and extensive service quarters.

In due course, the camp passed through several hands before becoming a private boys' camp. Sometime in the early 1950s much of the original camp was torn down, except for a guest cabin now part of the Wawbeek Hotel.

'A Quaint Lodge in the Country' — Adolph Lewisohn's Camp

IN 1904, *Town and Country* published 'A Quaint Lodge in the Country,' an article about an Adirondack camp. Located at Prospect Point on Upper Saranac Lake, the camp was designed by William L. Coulter for Adolph Lewisohn and built during 1903–04.

Coulter, who studied architecture at Columbia University, admired the work of Durant's Great Camps. His earlier works on both Upper and Lower Saranac lakes were rich with rustic decorative details, such as the log screens of Knollwood, and the half-timbering of the Kahn camp. To these examples he added his own ingenuity, talents, and love of foreign forms — such as the Japanese element, which is very strong in the Lewisohn design.

Coulter's original design sketch for Lewisohn's main lodge shows the debt owed to Durant's Sagamore Lodge. Under the long, sweeping gable roof, Coulter added the patterning of half-timbering, although the surfaces here are not covered with stucco but are sheathed with birch bark. Large racks of antlers in the gables are repeated symbolically in the crossed logs at the apex of the roof — identical, by the way, to a typical Japanese shrine detail.

Architect William Distin's 'Quaint Lodge in the Country' for Adolph Lewisohn at Upper Saranac Lake

The four main cabins
of Lewisohn's camp
were massive two-story
structures in the chalet
style. Richly textured
surfaces of Bavarian in-
spiration, using birch
bark to simulate stucco,
were juxtaposed with
patterns of log siding.
Main lodges were con-
nected by enclosed
walkways. Note the de-
tail of unpeeled
log siding on a
Lewisohn boathouse.

Two-story-high sitting room of a Lewisohn lodge, furnished in a mixture of styles.

The camp location originally included four thousand acres on a section of Upper Saranac Lake prestigious among the Jewish upper class, and already containing the camps of Otto Kahn and Isaac Seligman. Lewisohn lived on a grand scale and expected his homes to be luxurious. When he came for his month-long stay at camp, Lewisohn was accompanied by a staff of forty, including a major-domo, barber, caddy, chess player, singing teacher, and two chauffeurs. A colorful and lavish man who knew how to enjoy his wealth, he is reported to have spent about two and a half million dollars on his Adirondack camp from 1903 to 1930.

In the 1904 *Town and Country* article, Coulter said that Lewisohn permitted him 'to introduce striking effects and to execute all the fanciful ideas of rustic construction.' The architect's success in meeting his client's wishes are well illustrated in the original working drawings, contemporary photographs, and the well-preserved building on the site today.

Coulter's work and later additions by William Distin produced twenty-eight buildings ranging from the four main lodges linked by broad, enclosed passageways, to a boathouse and several smaller service buildings — all in little over a year, representing the largest effort yet seen in the Adirondacks and far exceeding any of Durant's logistical triumphs. Access roads did not yet exist, and material had to be brought down the lake from Saranac Inn, seven miles away; carpenters, stonemasons, plumbers, bricklayers, and blacksmiths worked through the winter producing many of the buildings' elegant details.

Although many of the details have been altered over the years, the boathouse in particular retains enough of the original work to present a virtual showcase for these labors. Located on the lakefront immediately below the main lodge, it was connected to the lodges by paths of crushed stone, rustic bridges and pavilions, and walkways lined with peeled log railings and an occasional rustic seat. A combination of half-timbering, birch bark, split poles, and rustic trim, the building was a mix of the Adirondack style and German architecture. It was simulated log construction; a broad overhanging roof with rustic-work brackets is the focal point of the building's design. The unusual chimney — a brick stack surrounded by logs — was removed in 1924.

The boathouse, main lodge, dining lodge, and west lodge are identical in exterior treatment with a lower story of log framing and upper

Adolph Lewisohn at his boathouse pier.

story of slab siding; the east lodge completed the next year differs in its exteriors of square timbers. These five principal buildings are similar in form, however, with broad, shallow-pitched roofs, large gables overhanging balconies and porches that face the lake, and half-timbering at the ground story.

Originally serving as Lewisohn's personal quarters, the magnificent main lodge is the largest building of the camp, connected by enclosed passageways to adjacent lodges. The lodge's focal point is the great gable of the central pavilion that faces the lake. Elevations are graced by a rustic circular porch, a first floor of spruce log-facing, balconies, and a projecting second floor of 'novelty siding' (spruce slabs). The gables are constructed of vertical split poles and bark sheathing, and projecting log bracketing supports the roof. As in other camp buildings and Great Camps of the early 1900s the spruce log-siding is notched and projects beyond building corners.

The original interiors of the main lodges were more conventional than the exteriors and luxuriously contradicted the rustic atmosphere. Proportions of most rooms are spacious, with high ceilings. Rusticity is limited in the numerous fireplaces, each of a unique design with overmantels of twig patterns or peeled logs, and, frequently, pebble hearths. Some rooms have exposed plank ceilings framed by peeled logs, matching the plank wainscoting of southern pine, while others have interior surfaces of cypress. The dining-room walls are finished in wide planks to a chair rail, with birch bark papering the walls and ceilings; ten-inch peeled logs frame the bark on the walls, and 16-by-18-inch logs on the ceiling. Other natural textures enlivened the interior surfaces; in the Lewisohns' bedroom, for example, walls were covered with linen to match the curtains.

The pride of workmanship is evident in the hardware, hinges, and even in the alignment of nailheads in planking. Interesting details abound: queen's-post roof trusses were exposed in several two-story spaces; windows in the dining room were pushed down into the floor to provide easy access to the porch; and staircases were of deliberately differing designs. Whether log or plank, wood joinery was superb. Ceiling lights and wall sidelights of wrought iron or copper, custom designed and fabricated on site, are located throughout the buildings. Originally, the lodges were decorated with Coulter-designed Arts-and-Crafts style furniture. One of the more unusual furnishings were some forty trash baskets formed of hollowed logs and embraced by stuffed bears, some of which remain.

The Lewisohn camp has had several owners since the first owner's death at Prospect Point in 1938. Despite use as private children's camps over the past forty years, the character of the camp has been respected: modest additions and minor maintenance renovations do not detract from its elegance. Much of the original splendor remains, although many of the decorative touches added by the furnishings have been lost. The stuffed bears have begun to deteriorate; the German newspapers used as taxidermy material can be pulled from worn spots. Most of the original linen wallcoverings are gone, yet the atmosphere that Adolph Lewisohn created is still present.

Unlike the modest scale of Knollwood, Lewisohn's camp, a luxurious collection of lodges, has all the key features of the idiom: a scenic location; a compound plan with individual buildings for separate functions; a variety of service buildings whose rustic design reflect their Adirondack setting. Their simulated, rather than true, log construction, their large scale, and the obvious hand of a professional architect are features particularly characteristic of the early twentieth century phase of the Adirondack building spirit.

TWO OTHER ELABORATE turn-of-the century camps are located on the southwest shore of Upper Saranac Lake. The dates of construction are lost but their grand scale remains intact. Sekon Lodge, the camp of Isaac N. Seligman, and Wenonah Lodge, built by Julius Bache, both illustrate the Great Camp tradition, one through rustic detail and the other in eclectic style.

Sekon and Wenonah

The Seligmans' Fish Rock Camp on Upper Saranac Lake is composed of six large cottages with broad roofs sweeping over porches and walkways.

The game room at Wenonah Lodge.

The Seligman camp is a picturesque collection of lodges on a magnificent site. A gradually sloping expanse of lawn permits sweeping views of the length of Upper Saranac Lake, to the north of the camp's main buildings, and of the camp itself from the water. Like Adolph Lewisohn's camp, Sekon was designed along the compound-grouping plan by William Coulter and built in the same period as Prospect Point camp. The complex is typical of a Great Camp tendency of the time to replace many small, single-purpose structures with fewer, large multi-function buildings.

The camp comprises over twenty major structures, including six lodges, two boathouses, smaller cabins, staff quarters, and support buildings. Although the six main lodges are large, they do not overpower the site. The sensitive spacing of buildings — building form and massing are uniform — repetition of prominent details, and unpeeled logs applied as exterior wall decoration provide continuity of design.

At Sekon Lodge, rapport with the woodland setting is masterfully achieved through the treatment of building exteriors: first floors are unpeeled log siding; bay-window projections soften the rectangular planes; and overhangs and porches with decorative railings adjust the buildings to the changes in grade. Second floors are shingled, with window openings paired and set in a panel of diagonal unpeeled logs. Ridge roofs have extensions over porches, projecting window bays, and lower-story wings.

A particularly striking feature used throughout Sekon is a roof known as a 'jerkinhead.' This form, which originated in southern Germany, is seen on every structure — as a gable or projection over a bay window, as a dormer roof, or as a visual emphasis on a passageway. It is even used as the entire roof for a boathouse and a tennis pavilion. Dimensions vary, depending on the building plan, but proportions are identical wherever the jerkinhead is used. A diagonal brace of unpeeled log is occasionally added to support the larger overhanging sections, repeating the same angle whether bracing roofs or porch columns. The jerkinhead is an effective architectural device, suggesting shelter, bringing buildings closer to the ground, and adding the same domestic scale to all structures. A subtler repetition of placement and proportions of window openings contribute to the overall camp aesthetic. Diamond-paned windows are typically grouped with doors, lightening the massive log structures.

Many of the original wooden walks and waterfront structures have been removed, but a delicate, hundred-foot-long footbridge extending from the shore to a small island once home to a jerkinhead pavilion is a reminder of the rustic ambience of the camp.

Fine plank wainscoting, with dyed burlap above the window heads to the ceiling, is used in several large interior spaces. The library of the main lodge has an unusual roof truss of unpeeled birch logs, spanning a floor space forty feet square.

Quite unlike the turn-of-the-century rustic camp that Coulter was evolving on Upper Saranac Lake, the camp of Julius Bache (here, the architect is unknown) was decidedly eclectic. A site smaller than the neighboring Seligman and Lewisohn camps results in a more compact complex of buildings. This density tends to emphasize the diverse architecture, from the Victorian to the Japanese. Camp buildings display a peculiar characteristic of 'sharp' edges because of the slab siding and roofs of red tile. One- and two-story main lodges have modified rustic elements — a wooden-membered screen in the gable of the main lodge — but the wood used is milled rather than rough-hewn.

Although eclectic, the camp achieves certain continuity through repetition of roof forms, color, and exterior siding. The use of square-cut timber for decorative framing, a unique feature, adds to the integration of the main lodge, guest cabins, boathouse, dining building, tennis shelter, and support buildings. Covered, connecting passage-

Above, *the scale of Sekon Lodge's main buildings was maintained by peeled logs, similar windows, and roofs blending with shingled upper stories. Left, dormers with jerkinhead roofs projected over gabled walls to a low overall building height. Below,* trusses of unpeeled birch logs in the library.

Above, *Bache's Wenonah Lodge, a camp built in the Victorian style. Teahouse overlooking Upper Saranac Lake is at center left. Below, Wenonah's main lodge, with boathouse and waterfront retaining walls, welcomed guests arriving by water. Right, the teahouse at Wenonah Lodge.*

ways complete the sense of unity. Slightly separated from the main camp is a small gazebo of strong Japanese influence. But even here, the carefully proportioned derivative design remains compatible with other camp buildings by use of square-cut framing timbers and a red tile roof.

In contrast to the diverse exteriors, interiors are quite properly rustic with varying wall-surface treatments. Paneling of peeled, split logs set between framing of peeled-log beams is used in the living room of the main lodge. Animal artifacts — heads and skins — are scattered throughout this room oriented to a massive rustic stone fireplace. In the main dining room and several other large rooms, walls are covered with birch bark and framed with unpeeled birch logs. Decorative hardware, lighting fixtures, and fireplace implements throughout the camp are executed in delicate black wrought-iron.

When the camp was built around 1915 it exhibited a clear departure from neighboring camps with their rustic exteriors, but continued the shift toward massive lodges and multifunctional camp buildings. The eclectic design of the unknown architect does not detract from the comfortable ambience of Bache's camp. The camp has borne up quite well over the years, and is now in use as a hotel called Winonah Lodge.

The Camp Era Ends

THREE OTHER CAMPS on Upper Saranac Lake designed by William Distin in the late 1920s carry on Durant and Coulter's earlier traditions in camp construction. Representing a culmination in Great Camp building, they complete the transition from delicately-scaled individual buildings to massive main lodges. With their construction the Great Camp era drew to a close, excepting a postwar Distin design for the Minnowbrook camp at Blue Mountain Lake.

Because of the depleted supply of suitable local spruce or cedar, logs had to be imported from outside the region. Logs eighteen and twenty-four inches in diameter were brought down from Canada for peeled-log siding, for decorative exterior framing, and for interior use. Manufactured windows and interior components diminish the rustic qualities but the architect and owners incorporated designs featuring the familiar tones and textures. In spite of the massive appearance of the main lodges, the style is informal and relaxed.

The first of these camps was built in the early 1920s at Indian Point on the east shore of Upper Saranac Lake. The site is accessible only by water and rises abruptly from the waterfront to a flat ridge. Two main buildings facing the lake are connected by a long covered passage spanning a ravine. One of the lodges served as the owner's cabin and

Although by the mid-1920s specimen logs for camp construction were scarce, selection for uniform taper and straightness still prevailed, as at the Day Camp on Upper Saranac Lake.

contains a living room and bedrooms; the other lodge contained a dining room, kitchen, recreation rooms, and guest rooms. Three other buildings were used for staff quarters and support services. The boathouse was also equipped with a recreation room on its second floor.

The main lodges seem deceptively great because of the use of large logs on exteriors. All surfaces are of a peeled spruce that over the years had developed a warm, yellow-red cast. Log-frame cabins of one and two stories rise from stone foundations to gables of vertically set, peeled spruce logs. Main walls are of notched, horizontal logs, again peeled, and with irregularly cut chamfered ends.

The architect's skillful use of vertical logs for porch skirting and in gables subtly varies the exterior textures, which are reinforced by the varied coloring of logs and plaster caulking. The peeled-log passageway and railings are of the same yellow-red. Smaller logs with branch stubs and knots bedeck railings, porches, and details of walks, boathouse, and dock. This selection of materials, probably due to unavailability of 'perfect' logs, would not have been used in the late-nineteenth-century Great Camp.

A suggestion of rustic comfort is barely visible to the passing canoeist.

lodges and support buildings. Proximity to the forest, warmth in the color of the exterior logs, and the modest interior give the camp its pleasant, relaxed mood. The transition from the outdoors to interior spaces has a unique naturalness. Now privately held, the two owners have divided the camp down the center of the main connecting passageway.

The second of the three camps built in the 1920s is an excellent example of the Adirondack Great Camp complex. Built on Markham Point, an isolated peninsula and accessible only by water, it represents the most popular image of the rustic camp. Gradual approach over the lake discloses a picturesque sequence of boathouse, log gazebo, and main lodge. The skill of Distin in absorbing the finest traditions of Durant and Coulter is expressed in this series of vignettes. Each successive detail of walkway, railing, and views is wonderfully orchestrated until the visitor is overwhelmed by the larger-than-life rustic screen of the main lodge. The massive log screen, no delicate fan placed in the gable, is used here to extend the end elevation from the porch floor to the roof support. The two-story, freestanding skeletal screen is repeated as a gable motif on a nearby guest cabin. Logs are used throughout, in the gazebo, the main lodge screen, and porches and railings. Exterior walls to roof lines and gables on the main lodge are of peeled-bark siding. Gables on the main lodge and boathouse are identical to the peeled-birch sheathing and log framing used by Coulter for the Lewisohn camp, which lies directly across the lake. Guest cabins, the boathouse, and several support buildings have horizontal plank siding to roof lines. The same width planking is turned vertically for the gables. A peculiar detail of projecting, square-cut timbers at building corners gives the illusion that the plank siding is actually a deep beam, similar in character to Swiss chalet construction of milled timbers.

Details Are Part of the Whole

From the main lodge, the two-story porch commands a sweeping view of the lake to the south and west, framed by the massive logs of the exterior screen. The porch leads directly into the living room, a crescendo in movement from water's edge through rustic building elements to interior space. The elegantly proportioned room with walls sheathed in wide planking rises a full two stories to a log-framed plank ceiling. A great fireplace of native stone in the wall opposite the porch is framed by stairways on either side that reach a balcony on the second-floor level. The staircases, open constructions of split, unpeeled logs, appear to be suspended in space. Tread surfaces and log ends are varnished to the same gloss as the plank interior surfaces. This treatment, an extension of the open, skeletal exterior screen, provides a subtle connection between indoors and outdoors. Wicker furnishings and rustic details decorate the main room.

161

*Interiors are as ele-
gantly simple as the
camp's porch screen.*

Above, *candlesnuffer octagonal roof at the entrance to the main lodge at Camp Wonundra. Left, an example of skilled craftsmanship in an arched stone doorway and log frame construction at Camp Wonundra. Below, a view from the lake.*

Floors, walls, and ceilings of wood carefully selected for graining and coloration are decorated with mounted game and Indian artifacts. The large windows, including sheets of plate glass, create an intimate relationship to the woodland surroundings. Over the years, owners have preserved the camp in its original condition.

The last of the three camps designed by William Distin stands on Whitney Point, an elevated, rocky, woodland site on a peninsula projecting into Upper Saranac Lake. Built from 1930 to 1933 for William Rockefeller, Camp Wonundra is an informal complex of nine buildings. This reduction in the number of buildings was typical of the post–World War I phase of Great Camp architecture. As with Distin's two other 1930-era Great Camps on Upper Saranac Lake, the main cabin is a large, multifunction structure.

The rocky nature of the site probably prevented earlier development as a camp location, but rapport with nature is a dominant theme of the camp and the site plan respects the boulder-strewn woodland setting. Paths, retaining walls, terraces, and building foundations are constructed of native stone. Few trees were removed and in fact terraces are built around especially fine specimens.

Camp Wonundra's rustic birdhouse of split-face logs.

Each building in the complex stands separate from others. The main lodge and guest cabin have impressive stone-foundation walls, log exteriors, and slate roofs. Native, cut stones are oversized; logs are eighteen to twenty-four inches in diameter. Broad overhangs and deep gables give a chalet effect to the main camp buildings. Details are bold and massive: the designer wisely avoided delicate rustic-work twig screens, which would have looked ludicrous in the rugged setting.

The eclectic main cabin at Camp Wonundra is one story high and contains a grandly proportioned living-dining room, two wings for bedrooms, and a service wing. Although the building is large, wide overhangs and an irregular silhouette keep it from appearing overpowering. The three rectangular wings and an octagonal vestibule radiate from the rectangular living-dining room. This angled-wing plan derives from shingle-style building of the 1880s, probably influenced by William Ralph Emerson whose work Distin included in his idea sketchbook. The architect also nods his head to the picturesque Queen Anne style, echoed in the irregular roofline and the vestibule. Unmistakably present are the inevitable inventions of Durant: the use of logs, rustic detailing, and the prominent gable.

Foundation walls of the main lodge and guest cabin are massive, native cut stone. Both buildings are constructed with halved logs of Canadian pine set horizontally, although corners have notched projecting logs suggesting true log construction. Progressions of logs project at the roof eaves and at the apex of the gables, a motif probably derived from Durant's work. The halved logs in the gables are peeled and set vertically. Most of the slate roofs have a gable shape, but the picturesque vestibule on the main cabin has the Queen Anne pyramid roof. Other interesting exterior features are metal window sashes, bay windows, wrought-iron hardware, and massive chimneys made of boulders.

The interiors of the main and guest cabins have the Great Camp casualness, a style underscored by confident superiority in workmanship and materials. Most of the floors are pegged wood. The walls and ceilings are covered with wide-board pine wainscoting. The elegant bathrooms, with their streamlined fixtures and black, white, and chrome color schemes, are unquestionably in the high style of the 1930s. These and other carefully conceived details, ranging from the imposing trusses in the living — dining room of the main cabin, to the spacious closets and custom-designed hardware, say much for Distin's design sensibilities.

Other buildings at Camp Wonundra include a boathouse, a log Adirondack lean-to, a stone pump house, a two-story garage-gardener's building, a one-car garage, a garage-woodshed, and a small sap house.

The use of log siding in the camp, even though the logs had to be imported from Canada, shows a deliberate continuation of the aesthetics of late-nineteenth-century Great Camp architecture. But except for one more Distin camp on Blue Mountain Lake built immediately after World War II, it was the last of its kind. Built in the Great Depression, though hardly its child, Wonundra closed the era of Great Camp building.

Above, *the architect's study for a stained-glass window at Camp Wonundra. Below, baronial living-dining room of Camp Wonundra's main lodge.*

Opposite, *Lake Placid from Camp Carolina.* Left, *the porches at Camp Santanoni.* Below, *the covered walkway at the Read Camp.*

CHAPTER 9

A CAMP IS A CAMP

Lieutenant Governor Timothy L. Woodruff provided a variety of diversions for Kill Kare's guests

EMOTENESS, isolation, insistence on privacy, and a vague public sense of hidden wonders have created the mystique of the
Great Camps. From Stoddard's description of 'artistic' cottages, over a century ago, to *Life* magazine's portrayal of Marjorie
Merriweather Post's regal posturings at Topridge, the public has had
an occasional glimpse of the number, size, diversity, and opulence of
the Adirondack vacation retreats. Barred roads and protective caretakers keeping the mystique of the camps intact act to increase public
interest when a private camp is opened to all or when state acquisition
permits public access to camps such as Santanoni or Nehasane.

Preservation of the remaining camps — about thirty-five of approximately 120 are in their original condition — requires a public policy
that identifies the best examples and determines, on a sound basis,
which will stay in private hands and which will become state property.
To increase public awareness, and to help set some guidelines for development of policy, ten extraordinary examples of Great Camps have
been brought together in this chapter, each representative of the finest
designs in the central Adirondacks. Located on private preserves of
hundreds to tens of thousands of acres, and predominately rustic in
character, each represents what its strong-willed owner was able to accomplish in the wilderness.

If there are two threads that suture this collection together, first is
their proximity to a railroad, and second is their common heritage of
the innovations of William West Durant. From Santanoni to Minnowbrook, they span six decades, from the Gilded Age through the end of
World War II. Early camps in this group were assemblages of cottages
après Durant, but expanded in size and interconnected to provide shelter for movement between buildings, while the late ones represent the
transition from cottages to massive family lodges, as architects refined
and reinterpreted owners' desires for gracious living in the forest.

The camps described in this chapter have been organized by date of
construction. All are in private hands, except Topridge and Nehasane,
which are owned by the State of New York, and all have been photographed as recently as 1980. That they have survived so long is a tribute to their builders, but the futures of several are in jeopardy, either
because the camps are the property of the state (Nehasane is expected
to be demolished), or because current owners are indecisive about dis-
position. Taken together, they underscore the need for definitive public policy on the preservation of the Great Camps.

A NEW YORK STATE Forest Commission report in 1893 described
'Camp Santanoni,' without comparison or qualifying comment, as
being well-designed and 'offering a remarkably fine example of what

Santanoni

Right, *exterior detail at Santanoni.* Opposite above, *service wing of the central lodge at Camp Santanoni. All the buildings are similar in construction, window openings, and roof forms.* Opposite right, *Santanoni's five main cottages are connected by 5,000 square feet of covered porches. Although the framing is separate from the buildings, the roofs are continuous.* Opposite left, *interiors of the cottages at Camp Santanoni were brightened by the admission of daylight onto varnished wood surfaces and dyed burlap wainscoting.*

can be done with rustic work in architecture.' The site that Robert C. Pruyn selected to start his building in 1888 covered over ten thousand acres, including Newcomb Lake, streams, ponds, and heavily wooded land. It was thirty-two miles from the railhead at North Creek and required building a road four and one-half miles long from the camp to the highway at the village of Newcomb.

A gatehouse and lodge located near the entrance, designed by the firm of Delano and Aldrich and added about 1910, introduces the visitor to the complex. Built of native stone, this first building group gives way to the access road. By skillful combination of culverts and bridges, the road traverses the rugged terrain with only modest changes in grade, opening vistas to streams and ponds along the way. Halfway to the main complex stands a group of support buildings constructed for staff and guides. Barns, houses, and sheds were located near clearings in the woods to furnish vegetable gardens and pasture for cows. The denseness of the forest screens the main complex until one is practically on top of it.

Pruyn's architect for Camp Santanoni was Robert H. Robertson of New York. Robertson, a member of the nearby Tahawus Club, created what at first appears to be a sprawling complex punctuated by open spaces between cottages. A black stain applied to the logs is reminiscent of the stave churches of Norway or structures of northern

Russia; the Imperial villa at Katsura, built in the mid-seventeenth century, may also have been an inspiration for Robertson. Bright red paint of all window and door frames relieves the somber nature of the dark logs and shadowed exteriors. Precise workmanship in the use of logs, the building massing, and the roof forms all sustain the impression of influences from other cultures.

Robertson selected a site on high ground, orienting the main complex to Newcomb Lake. The building plan itself is unusual in both concept and detail. A sophisticated roof system shelters the five cottages, an extensive network of covered verandahs tying them together. A kitchen building with staff quarters is attached to the cottages by a covered passageway, and an extension of the main roof forms a generous porte cochère.

Santanoni, as seen from Newcomb Lake, is composed about a formal axis that leads to a central pavilion rising above the flanking roofs. The inside of the central pavilion is dominated by a massive stone chimney with great fireplaces on opposite sides, one serving a lounge and the other a dining area. Split saplings applied diagonally within panels form wainscoting to windowsill height; walls and ceilings are papered with birch bark.

To the rear of the central pavilion is the detached kitchen building, itself an imposing log structure. Flanking the central pavilion are a pair of cottages stepping back from the pavilion and the lake. Each cottage contains a pair of units with sitting room, bedroom, and bathroom opening directly onto porches. The combined frontage of the main complex extends 265 feet, the interconnecting roofs and verandahs — over 5000 square feet of broad, wood platforms — containing impressive and rather cavernous exterior spaces.

A boathouse and a 'studio' building symmetrically frame the main-lodge complex. The rubble wall of the studio faces the lake and contains a twelve-foot-high arched window. To the rear of the kitchen building are several support structures, including a refrigeration building, and quarters for servants and guides. A constant water supply was provided by a spring on the site, and from it a complete system of plumbing served all the cottages ranged about the main lodge.

It is reported that for construction of the camp, over 1500 trees were felled and used for the buildings. Other building materials were taken directly from the site and the construction work performed almost entirely by men from neighboring villages. Even so, a minimum of forest was cleared, and trees came to the very edge of the building area.

The 1893 Forest Commission Report describes the camp: 'Although built of logs, the groups of cottages are well designed. . . .' and adds that there 'is so much rain in the Adirondacks, and life indoors is so

At Camp Santanoni's cottages, two-story gable screens are of openwork to admit daylight to porches and clerestory windows. Extraordinarily fine craftsmanship in the coping of framing logs, doors, and window openings distinguishes this early contemporary of Durant's camps, executed by the New York architect Robert H. Robertson.

unnatural, that provision against confinement was made by adding 5000 square feet of piazzas.'

The peeled logs used for framing and enclosing the cottages were first coated with an asphalt preservative, giving the unique coloration to the complex. This treatment has protected the exterior so well that there is no evidence of deterioration even after almost a century. In contrast to the dark logs on exterior walls, the peeled logs used to frame roofs were left unstained. The result is a heightening of the spaciousness of the roofed areas above the supporting walls. Railings and columns of unpeeled logs are large enough to provide a sense of support but are proportioned in relation to their function. Roof framing at gable ends is skeletal and transmits light to clerestory windows on interior building walls. This intricate exercise in rustic work is repeated at Camp Knollwood and other Saranac Lake camps, and in rustic architecture as far afield as national parks in the American West.

It is difficult to obtain overall vistas of the camp from either the ground or the air because of the dense surrounding pine forest. But even so, its delicate scale and unobtrusive presence in the wilderness is apparent. The Santanoni complex, epitome of refinement, has been adroitly fused by the use of roofs, verandahs, and coloring. The use of simple forms — enclosing walls treated as surfaces between roof and ground — along with a subtle adaptation to site and an elegant simplicity of details characterizes both the Adirondack camp and its Japanese counterpart, Katsura. Extensions of logs as definitions of building corners at Santanoni are executed in as fine a fashion as the intersections of columns and beams of the Oriental villa.

The fate of Santanoni is representative of the dilemma facing the Great Camps. When the Santanoni Preserve was acquired by the state of New York in 1970, no move was made to comply with the 'forever wild' mandate of the state constitution, which requires destruction of whatever buildings and facilities exist on an Adirondack site returned to the state. Presently, demolition is delayed, although maintenance is minimal. Santanoni, accessible by a five-mile hike or bicycle ride (motor vehicles are excluded), is now used as a public campground and is visited annually by about 2500 persons. Support to retain Santanoni has been strong enough to prevent its destruction, but its future remains tenuous.

Kamp Kill Kare

BASIC TO THE character of the Great Camps, as Anthony Garvan points out, is the sense of the improbable if not the impossible. This aptly describes the Garvan family retreat, Kamp Kill Kare. With Durant influencing the selection of the site and original buildings, and later expansion carried out by architect John Russell Pope, the camp was praised, in a 1903 newspaper article, as 'one of the most elaborate and picturesque in the mountains.' It has been expanded and maintained in exemplary condition since that early description.

The original Kill Kare preserve was part of Durant's Raquette Lake holdings. By the early 1880s he had built hunting lodges about two miles apart on what would later be the sites of Sagamore, Uncas, and Kill Kare.

In 1896 the State Forest Preserve Board purchased 24,000 acres from Durant. The sale included Sumner Lake, though a choice 1000-acre section around the lake in the middle of the tract was left out of the transaction. In 1898, Timothy Woodruff, lieutenant governor under Theodore Roosevelt and a member of the Board, turned up as

Aerial view of the Kamp Kill Kare main lodge and boathouse

the owner of that section, and changed the name of the lake to Kora. In 1899, a reporter of the *Albany Argus* described Woodruff's new camp as a 'palatial log home in the heart of the hills.' The writer, a former guest of Durant at the larger and more elaborate Sagamore, preferred Kamp Kill Kare as more 'unique and cozy.'

Another writer, Henry Wellington Wack, described in *Field and Stream* his 1903 visit to Sagamore, Uncas, and Kill Kare:

> I suppose these three camps . . . constitute in cost and comfort, in pleasurable appointments and in luxury, the finest trio on the North American continent. And I doubt if there is any forest villa in Europe to compare with either [sic] of them in any respect. Of the three, Kamp Kill Kare is by far the most picturesque and most completely furnished. . . .

In 1913 the camp was purchased by Alfred G. Vanderbilt and sold the next year to Francis P. Garvan. In 1915 a fire caused severe damage and John Russell Pope, better known for his Beaux Arts Classicism designs such as the National Gallery of Art in Washington, was called in by Garvan to help in the rebuilding. The Kamp Kill Kare of today is the result of this imaginative and continuous building campaign.

Left and opposite,
Kamp Kill Kare's mas-
sive main lodge, built
over many years and
influenced by Durant
and John Russell Pope,
is constructed in steps
down a ridge to
Lake Kora.

The scale of the camp is suggested by Pope's design of a monumental tower gate and extensive barn and service complex arranged
around an interior court. As one travels down the main entrance to the
camp, past the service complex, and through groves of pine trees
towering above clipped lawns, the lake eventually comes into view. A
guest house reposes offshore on an island. At this point, one drives
along the shore to the main complex, which extends along the lake.
Originally, as in other Great Camps, buildings were separated accord-
ing to function. Some isolated cottages still remain at the extremities
of the complex, although most of the major elements have been linked
together over time, creating a sprawling main lodge over three hundred feet long. The camp's informal character was supplemented by a
guest-boathouse complex, facilities for a large staff, and service buildings. At the end of the complex is a felicitous, and totally unexpected,
surprise: a diminutive but splendid stone chapel designed by Pope in
impeccable French Romanesque style.

The service areas of the camp display outstanding use of masonry
construction. The buildings, which included carriage, stable, and barn
facilities, a dairy, and woodworking, metal, and machine shops, were
designed by Pope into a U-shaped courtyard over two hundred feet

The exteriors and interiors at Kamp Kill Kare show the rustic in its lightest form. The siting of buildings, structure, rustic details, and furniture create a harmonious whole.

*The dining room at
Kamp Kill Kare.*

long on the inside face, entered through the tower gate. The fortress-like exteriors of rough-hewn granite quarried on the site yield cavernous spaces that are nonetheless carefully finished and detailed. The granite lintels alone, bridging wide barn doors, weigh several thousand pounds. The walls are often layered with alternating bands of rectangularly cut, flat stones and massive boulders. Round windows encircled by wedged slabs of granite are set triumphantly in the stony gables. Sheer massed weight of this precisely-cut masonry eliminated the need for mortar.

The roofs of the structures are framed in unpeeled logs that are also used for the detailing of dormer windows and other openings. Pope's magnificent use of stone is also seen throughout the main camp itself, particularly in the beautifully-executed fireplaces and chimneys that dominate many rooms of the camp.

Sitting on a hill, the main lodge is the focal point of Kamp Kill Kare, though it is so broken up in outline that its size is not easily grasped. Essentially a set of interconnected structures, never exceeding a story and a half in height, the lodge is built of fourteen-inch-thick logs, split, with flat sides exposed. From a distance, the camp appears to be an extremely active composition of horizontal and vertical elements rising in a long succession of low log forms from Lake Kora to the top of the ridge. As seen from the gabled ends, steeply pitched roofs rise against the sloping roofs of dormers. This play of shape contrasts with the polygonal roof forms covering octagonal rooms and porches. The whole composition marches along the landscape, constantly altering its elevation from above as well as from below as certain rooms are raised up and carried on their granite foundations.

Imposing though the array of buildings is in scope and setting, the interiors are the chief glory of Kill Kare. The owner's cabin, picturesque with its vine-covered entrance, is very likely the only 'pre-Pope' section of the main camp buildings still standing. A main bedroom ceiling of full two-story height was necessary to contain its unique furnishings and fireplace.

Although Pope's hand is evident in the magnificent dining hall spanned by massive timber trusses, much credit belongs to a retired British army officer named Hiscoe who visited the camp as a guest of the Woodruffs and assisted the Garvans in reconstructing the main building after the main lodge was destroyed by fire. He deliberately altered Pope's design, enriching the interiors with a consistent and disciplined use of twig designs and saplings. The rustic furniture assembled on the site is among the finest in the Adirondacks. Each room in the camp is decorated with trophies, Indian artifacts, and camp memorabilia.

Kamp Kill Kare, maintained today as a game preserve, is the most complete and self-sufficient of the Great Camps. From Durant's first small cabins through Pope's additions and renovations, Kill Kare has emerged as a masterwork of regional architecture, decorative display, and landscape art.

A main bedroom with rustic furnishings at Kamp Kill Kare.

Above, *William Seward Webb's Forest Lodge at Nehasane in 1894.* Right, *Forest Lodge in 1979.* Opposite, *an Adirondack lean-to on a ridge at Nehasane sheltered the owner's family from 125-mile-an-hour winds during a storm in 1950.*

ON THE SHORES of one of the Adirondack's most picturesque lakes, a   *Nehasane*
massive lodge sat silent and abandoned in the summer of 1980. As is
the case with Camp Santanoni, the lands of Nehasane Park and its Forest Lodge have been acquired by the state of New York for incorporation into the forest preserve. Although not of the extraordinary rustic
character of Santanoni, Forest Lodge is a magnificent representation
of the 'improbable if not the impossible' achieved by camp builders
challenging the wilderness.

William West Durant has been the understandable focus of much
attention for his influence on the opening of the Adirondacks and his
almost singlehanded creation of the 'artistic camp.' However, William
Seward Webb, builder of Nehasane, deserves equal credit for his successful construction of a railway, the Adirondack Railroad in 1891 and

1892. An article in the *New York Times* of January 1, 1895, described Webb's achievements:

> He built a thoroughly good railroad, equipped it in first-class style, and as now operated by the New York Central people, it is a source of health, comfort and pleasure to thousands of enthusiastic lovers of the North Woods. The Adirondack & St. Lawrence Railroad was not constructed in any common commercial spirit. For many years before the road was thought of W. Seward Webb was an enthusiastic frequenter of the Adirondacks. . . . Enjoying, as he did, thoroughly the beauties and health-giving qualities of this region, he also realized that comparatively few persons could gain access to it. . . . Dr. Webb had no idea of building simply a lumberman's road, although the lumbermen who ply this calling lawfully have been greatly benefitted by his enterprise. He built and equipped a first-class passenger railroad and his generous enthusiasm made the project a very expensive one. . . . Dr. Webb himself is the largest individual holder of Adirondack lands. He owns more than 200,000 acres. . . . It is to his interest to perpetuate and not despoil the Adirondacks. . . . One of the first things that a new visitor to the Adirondacks will ascertain, is the interesting fact that each and every person in the region considers himself or herself a personal friend of 'the doctor's.' W. Seward Webb is unquestionably the most popular man in the North Woods.

In his authoritative *Township 34* Harold Hochschild has said that Webb 'In opening new areas to recreation seekers, performed a great public service, as the Durants had done earlier.' Because Webb's railroad connected with the New York Central at Utica and so passed through the length of the Adirondacks to Malone terminating at Montreal, 'tourists, buyers of private camps, hunting and fishing clubs, hotel builders and lumbermen came tumbling into the Western Adirondacks in [his] wake. Lakes which had been one to two days travel from the nearest railroad found themselves within sight of the new line. Remote forest retreats blossomed into thriving summer resorts.' Soon a clamor arose to build railroads competing with Webb's to tap the Adirondacks' potential, but with these commercial rumblings came an attendant counterdemand for protection of the northern wilderness. By 1894 the famous provision, later amended as Article XIV, created the forest preserve as 'forever wild,' placing it under the protection of a state constitution that can be modified only through an exhausting process.

Left, *the living room of Forest Lodge contains a player piano;* below, *stuffed bears cavort on the rustic fireplace.*

*Shingle Style
Architecture in
the Adirondacks*

After construction of his railroad through the Adirondacks was completed — in only eighteen months — Webb turned his attention to building his personal estate. A site was selected a short distance from Webb's own railroad station on the shore of Smith's Lake, renamed Lake Lila in honor of his wife, the daughter of William H. Vanderbilt. Webb selected as his architect Robert Robertson, the designer of Camp Santanoni. The architect, who had previously designed other projects for Webb at Shelburne, Vermont, was on a fishing trip at Nehasane Park when he died of a heart attack in 1896.

Unusual in Great Camp design, the main lodge presents a fine example of 'shingle style' architecture. No rustic work is incorporated in the design — the building would not have been out of place at fashionable seaside resorts of Newport and Bar Harbor. The massive roof forms and expressive dormers extend to shelter verandahs running the length of the family wing facing the lake. Oculus windows, 'eyebrow' dormers, and red-brick chimneys incorporated in the design are characteristic of the shingle style. The arrangement of building massings and the style and execution of detail all bear witness to the influence of contemporary work by H. H. Richardson, and McKim, Mead and White.

The main lodge is a spacious structure containing enormous living and dining areas graced with large, native-fieldstone fireplaces. The living room, two stories high, is a well-proportioned space, furnished and decorated with hunting trophies. The lodge had accommodations for twenty-five people, including eight to ten guides. An additional eleven cabins housed guests and had space for a staff of ten servants. There were two kitchens, one catering to family and guests and the other to guides and servants. Two boathouses were part of an extensive shoreline development of stone retaining walls.

Outlying buildings, including barns, guest cabins, and boathouses, harmonize with the massive, asymetrical main lodge. Shingles sheath all exterior surfaces. Windows, of equally generous proportions, contain a central pane surrounded by square, smaller ones. Interior surfaces of vertical pine beaded-wainscoting are varnished to a high luster.

Dr. Webb's original holdings comprised over 225 square miles, but the maintenance of control over such a vast area was difficult. In 1895 he disposed of a large part of his nonwaterfront holdings, selling 75,000 acres to the state. Later he sold off all but 40,000 acres and created the Nehasane Park Association as a private game preserve. He fenced in about 10,000 acres around Lake Lila with a woven-wire fence ten feet high, and stocked the enclosure with moose, elk, and black-tailed deer. In 1896 Webb hired Gifford Pinchot, the distinguished forester and conservationist, to create a forest-management plan similar to the one created in 1892 for his brother-in-law, George Vanderbilt at Biltmore, North Carolina. Pinchot later became the first chief of the U. S. Forest Service and the governor of Pennsylvania.

In the summer of 1979, 25,000 of the remaining 32,000 acres of the park were acquired by the state of New York. The transaction was a complex arrangement including outright acquisition of a portion of the land, and retained use of the balance with easements for a period of fifty years by family members. The Adirondack Conservancy purchased the property from Webb heirs 'holding' the land until state funding could be arranged for the purchase. Lands now accessible to the public have been enormously improved through the Webb family stewardship of eighty-five years. But the addition of the Nehasane land to the Adirondack Park assures the camp's eventual demolition. Perhaps because the buildings are not considered architecturally or historically outstanding, or because other, more devastating, demolitions are contemplated, no public outcry has yet been voiced for their style is actually more appropriate to the seashore than the wilderness. Its destruction is still a sorry precedent.

Keepawa station on the Adirondack Railroad.

Above, *the main lodge at the Read Camp, Little Simon Pond.* Right, *covered passage connects the Read Camp main lodge to the dining room.* Opposite, *the Read Camp dining room is perched on a massive outcropping projecting into the lake.*

FOR MANY of the camps described in this book, only scanty records are available concerning the camp's beginnings. Original owners and builders are dead; anecdotes conveying the sense of the early years of ownership are few. On a few occasions, a camp's cultural heritage has been imperfectly preserved in anecdotes recorded elsewhere or in interviews of people associated with a camp's early owners or builders. In rare instances, some architectural sketches have survived. However, we are fortunate in having a thorough record of at least one.

The William A. Read camp, completed in 1906, was described in a contemporary architectural journal, *American Architecture and Building News* (1906), and in *House and Garden* (December 1907). Both articles give a thorough picture of the camp shortly after construction. But more important, the originality and uniqueness of this vernacular architecture was heralded in national magazines committed

'An Adirondack Lodge'—The Read Camp

189

to illustrating the tastes and styles of the period. *House and Garden* described the camp:

> A comfortable night's travel on the Adirondack Montreal Express from New York and a seventeen mile drive through the woods, takes one to the beautiful mountain lake in the heart of the Adirondacks on which this camp is situated. The site is an ideal one in every way. The lake affords excellent boating . . . furnishes an unfailing supply of purest water for the camp as well as a home for the brook trout with which it abounds.
>
> The estate is composed of 5,000 acres of woodland entirely surrounding the lake and extending to the summit of the adjoining ridges, which rise almost perpendicularly from its shores. From the top of one of these, Mount Morris, 3700 feet above the sea, a most wonderful view of the surrounding country can be obtained, including some fifty different bodies of water.

In 1905, Read commissioned the New York architectural firm of Davis, McGrath and Shepard to create a woodland retreat. The camp, now six miles from the highway by a dirt access road, is sited on a knoll projecting well into the lake. The main lodge, about thirty feet above the lake, contains the living room and sleeping quarters, while the dining room, kitchen, and servants' quarters are placed about two hundred feet away on a rocky point projecting some distance into the lake and about twenty feet above it. The two buildings are connected by a rustic covered passageway, that adjusts to the grade through use of two flights of steps with a square pavilion midway.

The Architect's 'Picturesque Effect'

House and Garden described the 'picturesque effect': 'There has been no attempt made at landscape gardening, but rather an effort to leave the grounds in a natural state, and preserve as far as possible all natural grades.' On the opposite side of the camp was a boathouse, stable, guide house, reservoir, pump house, and a wood shed. About a half mile away was a curling rink, noteworthy in that it attests to winter use of a camp. Spaces created by the log construction are covered with a light-colored Portland cement over strips of wire lath. Peeled logs were stained with a dark-brown wood preservative. Buildings are well-defined by their symmetry and precision in extended notched logs at each corner. Projecting gable ends, broad overhangs, corbeled logs, and scrolled brackets add a Swiss touch to the design, further emphasized by vertical-plank balcony railings and stepped corner logs at the foundation and roof supports. Stuccoed gable ends add a final Swiss embellishment.

The rustic effect of peeled logs is employed in porches and railings, diagonal braces, and massive fireplaces of native stone. The main lodge is 'floated' above the irregular natural grade by a stone foundation, which provides a natural transition to the ground floor logs. Where the grade drops sharply towards the lake, log coursing without plaster chinking is used as a foundation wall in combination with native stone. Stepped logs at building corners and a porch with a rustic railing on three sides also successfully separate the main building masses from the grade. Although the main lodge is two stories high, alternating bands of dark logs, white plaster chinking, and windows with white-painted sashes lighten the massive volume of the building.

The owner's desire (described in *House and Garden*) not to disturb the natural setting required that:

Harmony with the Environment

> The logs for the various buildings [ten-inch-diameter spruce] were cut from the surrounding forests, each one selected with great care as to size, and more particularly to location, not more than one tree being taken from any one spot, so that its loss would not be noticed from the lake. The stone for the foundations, chimneys, etc., was all quarried from the mountainside in out-of-the-way places.

Finished materials were brought in over snow and ice before construction began, and during construction the contractor erected a temporary camp with kitchen, dining room, and sleeping quarters for the forty or more workers.

The plan of the two-story main lodge is H-shape, with overall dimensions of forty-five by ninety feet. A living room twenty-five by forty feet is entered from a deck sheltered by the overhanging main roof. At one end is a wide rustic staircase and a great rustic stone fireplace; at the other end, a raised alcove with cushioned seats. The ceiling is constructed of solid-hewn beams — showing the axe marks — with chamfered edges, supported on hewn posts with corbeled brackets. The wall panels formed by the posts and studs, also hewn, are filled in with burlap. All exposed wood is stained dark brown.

Three spacious bedrooms and a gun room, each with different fireplace and mantel treatments, are located in the wings of the ground floor, flanking the living room and opening directly onto the broad decks surrounding three sides of the building. The second floor contains six additional spacious bedrooms, whose walls and ceilings are finished in a natural spruce, paneled and stained in a variety of soft colors. Corner bedrooms facing the lake have private balconies, three of the six rooms have private bathrooms, and five of the six rooms have fireplaces. Windows throughout are single sash, hinged at the sides, with small panes 'such as are always to be found in the old log cabins and a considerable part of the quaintness of the camp is due to this feature' (*House and Garden*, 1907).

A corridor connects the living room to the deck on the west side of the main lodge. Steps down from the deck lead to the covered walkway raised aboveground on posts and open to the forest on both sides: this serves as a connection between living room and dining room. It is here that the walkway widens to accommodate a bench and a resting place overlooking the lake.

The dining room is a large octagonal room, twenty-five feet in width and open to a roof supported by heavy hewn trusses. The upper part of the room is lit by a circle of small clerestory windows, which can be opened for additional ventilation. Directly below these windows and above the wood wainscoting are large panels papered with burlap. Opposite the main entrance to the dining room is a fireplace, six and a half feet wide and five feet high.

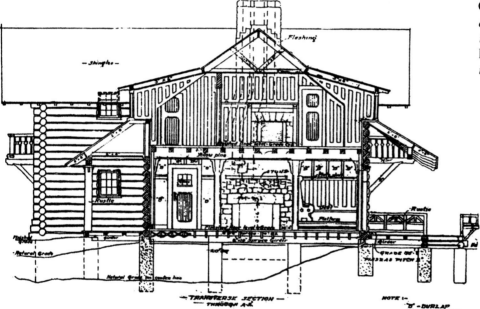

Opposite, *rich details of the Read Camp seen in place today and,* left, *on the architect's drawings of 1906.*

In the pages of the *American Architect* for the year 1906, residential architecture is represented by sprawling shingle mansions, Normandy cottages with stucco exteriors, and townhouses in New York City and Washington presenting elegant stone façades to the street. The same year's issue also carries photographs and plans of New York's Pennsylvania Station, High Gothic cathedrals in Newark, New Jersey, equestrian statues, and cemetery gateways. The influences were as eclectic as the Beaux Arts could provide. Astonishingly, the Davis, McGrath and Shepard lodge for Read expresses a solidly independent taste and style not at all overwhelmed by such ponderous competition.

Any notion that the Read lodge is a simple, unsophisticated log cabin is quickly dispelled by an inspection of the working drawings. Contemporary residences would have had the same foundations of poured-in-place concrete; milled 6″ x 10″s; 3″ x 8″s for structural

The main lodge of the Kildare Club at Jordan Pond. Opposite, polygonal forms housing the large public rooms of the Kildare Club project from the main building mass. The Club's main lodge exteriors are covered with unpeeled cedar logs; a horizontal lower course of logs rises to the windowsills and a vertical upper course to the roof eaves.

framing of walls, floors, and roofs; and heating, plumbing, and electrical systems. The camp differs from contemporary eclectic residential construction in the application of entire peeled logs for veneers on exterior walls. Building interiors are further detailed in a fine wainscoting or framing for burlap wall-covering.

The designers' intention of conveying a rustic flavor is shown by notes on the drawings and by the letter 'H' identifying hewn logs. Diagonal braces providing balcony and roof supports are labeled 'rustic.' The design drawings also help in interpreting other influences: the classical symmetry of building massing, exterior openings, and spaces; and Queen Anne style organization of gables, dormers, and balconies.

However, in the synthesis of these different styles, the 'picturesque' is always in evidence. For example, the Swiss embellishments, the light bands of plaster against stained logs, and the placement of porches and balconies, add grace to the massive bulk of the building.

In its time, the Read camp was unique among its Beaux Arts contemporaries. The sheathing of logs under a broadly sheltering roof could only belong in a dense forest. To walk on a covered walkway between main lodge and dining room, viewing forest and lake miles from

any other people or buildings; to ascend stairs on massive granite out-croppings on the way to an elegant dinner were part of the 'improbable if not impossible.'

Preserved by the Read family today, this Great Camp reaches back to an era of great land holdings and achievement — creation of a unique architecture in the woods.

BUILT IN THE same year as the William A. Read camp, the Kildare Club was also in the rustic Adirondack style and set on a private preserve. The original preserve of almost ten thousand acres was formed as a hunting and fishing club in 1892 by William Seward Webb, Frederick W. Vanderbilt, and several others. The only access to the rough hunting lodge of earlier years was by foot or horseback on a crude wagon road seven miles from the settlement of Hollywood on the Raquette River. In 1896 the club was purchased by the family of the present owners. After a fire destroyed the hunting lodge, a permanent complex was designed by the Saranac Lake architects, Scopes and Feustman; construction was completed in 1906.

Kildare Club

195

The complex of twenty-five buildings that now forms the Kildare
Club does not have any association with organizations similar to the
Adirondack League or Ausable Club. Its use has always been as a private family camp, making even more impressive the dedication to
stewardship of the natural environment. The 1893 New York State
Forest Commission Report notes that the Kildare Club, originally assembled by Webb in 1880, did not permit timber cutting on any of its
land. The fishing was described as excellent and the abundance of
game as unsurpassed in the Adirondacks. The club as it exists today is,
in effect, a Canadian zone wild-life preserve.

A mile from a side street in the village of Tupper Lake, the visitor
passes a gatehouse and then begins an extraordinary journey to the
main camp on a single-lane, unimproved road through sixteen miles of
what is practically virgin forest. The private preserve consists of two
tracts: one, of 4500 acres, was logged for selected white pines, possibly
for ships' masts, during the Civil War. No other removal of trees has
occurred since then. On the second tract, of over 5400 acres, some selective logging occurred after World War II as part of a forest management silvicultural project. To avoid disrupting the forest of evergreens
and hardwoods, cable has been buried alongside the road rather than
strung aboveground — all at the owners' expense. In this setting, all
mammals native to the Adirondacks (except for the timber wolf,
moose, and panther) have survived.

As one travels into the Kildare Club there is little question why
Philip Wylie chose it as the site for the last stronghold of civilization in
his futuristic novel *The End of the Dream.* Wylie had been a guest at
the Kildare Club and is remembered for his ability to call the loons
from the lake to the edge of the dock.

The main-lodge complex represents the shift in Great Camp planning at the turn of the century. A two-story main lodge incorporates
living, dining, recreation rooms, and family bedrooms in a single
structure. Family cottages and guest cabins provide additional accommodations. The land surrounding the complex is heavily wooded and
slopes gently toward Jordan Lake, one of the two large private lakes in
the preserve.

The main buildings are wood frame with spruce log siding; ends of
the split-log veneer are cut square at building corners. Horizontal
coursing runs from grade to window sills, and from sill to roof the unpeeled logs are placed vertically. This motif, carried throughout the
camp, was adapted from earlier buildings on the site, one of which,
with its plaster chinking, is still in use as a service structure.

Rustic touches are added elsewhere on the main lodge as exterior-
log porch details, diagonal braces, and balconies. Dining and billiard
rooms are striking and spacious. The dining room has an unusual ceil-

ing of peeled bark, from which is suspended a dramatic chandelier of stag horns. The billiard-room ceiling is a vault of narrow wooden planks with highly varnished surfaces.

Like many of the early camps, Kildare Club originally was comprised of temporary tent platforms which were eventually replaced. A curiosity of the complex is a building which, though resembling a tent platform in appearance, is constructed of permanent materials.

Like other Great Camps set in private preserves, the Kildare Club illustrates the happy coexistence of woodland conservation and architectural preservation. Of course, within a tract of ten thousand acres, man's impact on the surroundings can be easily disguised. The entry road and the campsite themselves are only a tiny fraction of the total land holdings. Disruption of the woods has been minimal, and the costs borne privately to accomplish these ends. Forest management at Kildare has been conservative — that is, little of the mature forest growth has ever been removed. On similar preserves — such as the contiguous Nehasane, Whitney, and Litchfield holdings of over 100,000 acres — a stewardship emphasizing the preservation of natural resources has been practiced for generations.

As part of the Adirondacks' cultural heritage, the Kildare buildings are an excellent example of rustic Great Camps. But even more important, the visitor can travel through virgin forests and a wildlife preserve. The Kildare Club presents a paradigm for preservation of the privately owned Great Camps set in ever-receding wilderness.

An Era Comes to a Close

IN THE mid-1920s, the era of the Great Camps was reaching its final stages. Main lodges with clusters of support buildings were being created for camp owners by the matured talent of local architects and the designs of eminent architects of the East Coast establishment. Vast acreage assembled earlier for modest prices was being put to use by the wealthy who had decided that the time to build in the Adirondacks had arrived.

A large parcel of land was still desirable for privacy, but efforts to create a complete environment in the wilderness soon faded and vanished under the impact of the first World War. Assembling large land holdings and building Great Camps would continue on to the Depression, but as opulent lifestyles diminished, the era of the Great Camps drew to a close.

Two Great Camps built in 1913 and a third in 1916 represent the diversity of site selection, design, and owners' tastes. One of these, Camp Carolina, was built on a small preserve of 125 acres at the north end of Lake Placid. It was surrounded by state land and was accessible only by a two-mile boat ride. A second camp, a tribute to local handi-

An aerial view of the Litchfield Chateau.

work, was built for the owner of the Santa Clara Lumber Company with land holdings of over 100,000 acres. A third is a chateau whose unrivaled grandeur and elegance make substantial claim for it in the heritage of Adirondack architecture.

Camp Carolina

THE VILLAGE OF Lake Placid has become famous as the setting for two Olympic Winter Games. Earlier, the area was famous for a farmer who eventually left to pursue his abolitionist goals: John Brown of North Elba. The beauty of the mountains and lakes that had originally attracted Brown also brought summer visitors. By 1872, camps were being built on Lake Placid and hotels around Mirror Lake.

The setting and its camps were lauded in Wallace's guidebook of 1894:

> Lake Placid as a pleasure-resort has a very select following and the best social elements have here full sway. It is mostly a rendez-vous of a refined and wealthy class of tourists . . . and now that railroad communication is established, it may safely be prophesied that the day is not far distant when it will have become one of America's most popular watering-places. It already attracts annually thousands of visitors. The sumptuous cottages of many of these, in chosen places, adorn the richly wooded banks of Lake Placid as well as the shores of Mirror Lake.

By the turn of the century over one hundred camps had been built on the shores of the five-mile-long lake. The Lake Placid camps were built on a smaller scale, though more densely, than were their neighbors of Saranac Lake to the west. Also, the Lake Placid camps were more noticeably similar in architectural style and general siting than those of neighboring lakes because of the common denominator of a few part-time contractors who worked together on many of the camps.

Lake Placid soon became known as 'Peerless Placid' and the 'Gem of the Adirondacks.' In Seneca Ray Stoddard's guidebook of 1904, he gave this description:

> Many places offer as their natural attraction a single lake, bit of forest, or mountain. Some have two of these features; Placid has all three, at their best: two of the most beautiful American lakes, virgin forests near on every side and literally scores of mountains within a day's walk, any one of which would make the reputation of an ordinary resort.

It may well have been this description that attracted Caesar Cone, the textile-mill owner of North Carolina, to the spectacular 125 acres

Lake Placid and the High Peaks frame the dock of Camp Carolina.

that nestles below Mt. Whiteface at the northeast corner of Lake Placid. Surrounded by state lands, the site can be reached only from a landing two miles across the water. A view from this landing fixes on the pale scar of Mt. Whiteface, setting the camp against a backdrop of forest and mountain. A distant composition of clustering buildings is slowly revealed as a picturesque complex of ten structures. A boathouse and dock stand at water's edge and a main lodge perches midway up the steeply sloped site. Although the land has been cleared in front of the main lodge, the land behind remains heavily wooded.

The two-story main lodge and the original 125-acre site made Camp Carolina one of the largest camps on the lake. Max Westhoff of New York City, who became a partner of Coulter, designed the buildings in 1913 to provide a comfortable summer home of eighteen rooms. Construction, of wood-framing with a shingled exterior, was supervised by George Bola, and executed by the local contracting firm of Arthur and Hayes. The front elevation rises from a foundation of native stone to an eight-foot-wide porch, articulated by a raised roof of open-timber framing at the entrance, and repeated in gabled dormers of similar shape. Rustic touches of peeled logs are added to porch details, balcony railings, and stucco on gable ends. But the large number of window openings, grouped together and emphasized by wide trim painted white against the brown shingles, suggest a suburban country home rather than a rustic camp.

The main lodge's interiors are of finely detailed wood used throughout on all surfaces. Daylight, from the many windows, reflects on the varnished surfaces. A 33-foot-long living room has horizontally laid log walls, a beamed ceiling, and a huge stone fireplace. A splendid cantilevered staircase of peeled and polished split logs rises to the next story. There are nine double bedrooms for the family upstairs, and a four-bedroom servants' wing. A separate building contains a laundry and additional sleeping rooms for staff. A copy of the original furnishings list itemizes rustic pieces scattered throughout the first floor and fine oak furniture by White Furniture and Heywood & Wakefield in the bedrooms. The sophisticated mission-style furnishings were the work of Gustav Stickley.

The complex as it exists today is still in private hands, with all furnishings marvelously intact.

The Meigs Camp

ONE OF THE largest owners of Adirondack land at the turn of the century was the Santa Clara Lumber Company, which at one time held over 100,000 acres of woodland, with holdings spread over several counties. An attractive setting owned by the Company was at Point-of-Pines on Big Wolf Lake near the village of Tupper Lake. Several log

Camp Carolina under the shadow of Mount Whiteface, with boat-houses and the funicular for carrying deliveries up to the main lodge.

buildings existed on the site in 1916 when the president and chief owner of Santa Clara, Ferris Meigs, chose it for his personal camp. Selecting a high point of land commanding a choice view of the lake, he set about building an unpretentious summer home.

It was a particular privilege in 1979 to hear Meigs's daughter, Lucia Meigs Andrews, describe the building of the camp as she recalled it from her childhood.

When Mr. Meigs wanted his own camp built to plans he'd drawn himself, his lumberjacks held a competition for the honor of building for the 'boss'. Franz DuPlante and his crew were the winners and went to work under the close supervision of Fred LeBoeuf, the company's head woodsman, an unlettered but naturally gifted builder and engineer. Those men cut well matched logs, peeled them clean in the woods, flattened both sides of each log using only hand tools, fitted them exactly together, even bevelled the exposed ends.

Experts have admired their craftsmanship which stands without flaw after sixty-three years. The main entrance doors have no metal parts and were made entirely by hand. Their wooden hinges and latches, with squeaks and groans, give early warning signals of arriving visitors.

Above, *Christina Kaiser at the Meigs Camp's original water supply.* Right, *Meigs lumberjacks became carpenters skilled in fitting and joining framing, producing some of the finest log work in the Adirondacks.*

Above, *the rambling main cabins of the Meigs Camp are two-story-high log-framed buildings. Shingled dormers and bay windows were later modifications. Left, a door without metal hardware. Far left, cedar corner post of the Ferris Meigs camp, placed on the foundation stone in 1913.*

The camp consists of a compound of log buildings, including a main lodge, several guest cottages, boathouse, and staff buildings. Workmanship has weathered well, and even though a few alterations have modified building exteriors, the original camp and its furnishings are intact. Memorable sunsets and the beauty of countless summer evenings have provided several generations of the Meigs family and their guests with pleasures the Adirondacks never fail to bestow.

The Litchfield Chateau

IF KAMP KILL KARE can be considered the paragon of the rustic Great Camp, then the Litchfield Chateau is an example of the most fanciful. Viewed from the air, or at a mile's distance from its private lake, the retreat created by Edward H. Litchfield may be challenged for drama only by Vanderbilt's Biltmore in North Carolina. The massive construction, extraordinary interior spaces, and elegant detailing challenge the imagination, only to inspire wonder at such an accomplishment in so remote a location.

Litchfield, a lawyer from Brooklyn who had prospered in land development, first came to the Adirondacks for camping and hunting in 1866. Like many wealthy men of the time, he often traveled the world

Litchfield Chateau from the air.

to hunt wild game. It was 1893 before he returned to the North Woods to establish Litchfield Park. He bought 8600 acres and then enclosed the tract with a wire fence eight feet high. His purpose was to stock the park with wild game and to breed them under natural conditions, but the plan was ultimately doomed by breaks in the fence, severity of the climate, disease, and poachers.

In 1911 Litchfield retained the New York architect Donn Barber to design a summer retreat. For two years, teams of laborers worked on access roads, landscaping, and construction of the chateau, the work force reaching a highpoint of six hundred. By 1913, construction was brought to an end. A five-mile-long road had been built from the settlement of Moody to the estate. Another fifteen-and-a-half miles of scenic carriage roads were built within the park.

The chateau is reminiscent of medieval architecture and would not be out of place in the south of France or in Germany. The skillfully landscaped access road brings the visitor through the forests, permitting a tantalizing glimpse of the chateau across the full length of the lake. The startling sight of a stone tower topped by a pyramid roof at the side of the great main building, with terraced levels stepping down to the lakeshore, is quickly obscured again by a screen of trees. Donaldson noted:

Modern Structure in a Medieval Shell

> Surrounded by the great forest, backed by billowy masses of primeval trees, this fortress of a modern fancy looms up on the lonely lake with an old-time splendor and a bygone beauty. It reminds one of those castles of delight that Ludwig of Bavaria was wont to conjure up in the remotest depths of his royal woods.

Once through the forest, one emerges at a gateway flanked by pillars and marble lions. A hundred-yard entrance drive cuts through soaring pines and clipped lawns, terminating in the triple arches of the main entrance to the chateau. In the original design, the tower left of the entrance was to have been repeated on the right side.

The chateau is constructed of steel and reinforced concrete and surfaced with granite — exterior walls are from three to six feet thick. The stone surfacing was taken from three quarries on nearby Mt. Morris, providing the variety necessary for a harmonious and impressive whole. Floors throughout are of marble or tile; wherever wood paneling and mahogany trim were used, they were applied as a covering over fireproof structural materials.

The ground floor contains various public rooms, all spacious in proportion and made comfortable by warm finishes and appropriate furnishings. A two-story library in the main tower has a massive fireplace and contains several thousand volumes. One of the most extraordinary

spaces in the chateau, and in all of the Adirondacks for that matter, is a vast hall — thirty feet wide, thirty feet high and sixty-five feet long. Walls are covered with a wainscoting of mahogany paneling to a height of twelve feet, exposing granite above. Hung along the walls are 160 of the Litchfields' game trophies from all over the world: lions, zebras, elephants, hippopotami, water buffaloes, giraffes, and a variety of deer along with several grizzly bear skins as rugs. A musician's balcony overlooks two suits of armor guarding the entrance at one end of the hall; at the other end is a fireplace fifteen feet high and six feet wide, with an antique mantlepiece superbly filigreed in gilt.

Other rooms contain a number of authentic antique fireplaces, garnered from old chateaux and castles in England and France. All of the corridors are decorated with deer or stag horns, mostly foreign; several main-floor galleries provide views of the lake and forest. An on-site gasoline-powered plant produced the electric power necessary for such an overwhelming structure; a coal-burning furnace provided steam heat. The power house, garages, a boathouse, and a greenhouse have been built in the same style as the main lodge. Elsewhere on the property are a large shooting lodge and caretaker's compound.

For many years after acquiring the preserve, Edward Litchfield avoided cutting any of the forest except for firewood and repurchased some outstanding leases from loggers. With the advent of the federal income tax law in 1913, many with large private landholdings suddenly faced a choice: either sell some of their land to reduce the cost of carrying the balance, or incorporate it as a business venture. In 1924, the 28,000-acre estate became the Litchfield Park Corporation. To prove its commercial intentions, the corporation began to harvest the spruce, which had stood uncut since the 1890s.

From that time on, the Litchfield family has worked diligently to preserve the park, leasing to clubs for recreational purposes and instituting forest management programs. Selective cutting and careful game management by the hunting and fishing clubs have preserved the woodland values of the park. Making the land profitable enough to offset taxes without violating the goals of preservation and conservation is a precarious business, and the current status of Litchfield Park is a tribute to one family's stewardship. The question facing Litchfield Park and other private preserves is whether such a sensitive balance can be maintained in the future.

A FLAMBOYANT WOMAN of enormous verve and energy, Mrs. Marjorie Merriweather Post Close Hutton Davies May never did things in half measures. Heiress to the Post Cereal Corporation fortune after her father's death in 1914, she built the company into the General Foods

Opposite below, *the great hall of Litchfield Chateau with walls adorned with trophies. A Stanford White-designed fireplace with a French medieval mantelpiece.* Opposite above, *the towers of the Chateau rise above massive stone walls.* Above, *suit of armor and trophies in the great hall.*

Topridge

Upper St. Regis Lake from the Topridge dock on an early summer morning.

Corporation through a series of skilled mergers. Her daughter, the actress Dina Merrill, relates that during her mother's marriage to Edward Close, Marjorie was the guest of friends on Upper St. Regis Lake. In 1920, newly married to the broker Edward F. Hutton, she acquired the steep hogback ridge that gives Topridge its name and set about converting the then modest camp, accessible only by water, into the present complex of sixty-eight buildings. On its east side the ridge drops off dramatically to a bay of Upper St. Regis Lake, dipping on the west to Upper and Lower Spectacle ponds. Mrs. Post began work there in 1923 to provide a retreat that would be as comfortable as her Fifth Avenue mansion and elegant estates in Washington, D.C., Palm Beach, Long Island's North Shore, and a 16,000-acre South Carolina plantation.

When fully occupied, Topridge had a staff of about eighty-five. Staff buildings on the grounds tell a story in themselves. There are thirty-two rooms in two buildings for maids, cooks, and their assistants — separate cabins with living rooms, kitchens, bedrooms, and baths. Mrs. Post maintained about seven guides on staff. While they swept walks and did other maintenance chores, they were also on call if any of her guests wanted to fish, go for a walk, or have a cookout at the lean-to at the lake's shore.

Guests arrived by private plane or were brought by chauffeured limousine to St. Regis Lake, where they boarded a 26-passenger yacht for the trip to a private dock at the end of the lake. From the landing, a funicular took them up the hill to Topridge.

Original designs for the camp were prepared for Mrs. Post by a firm of New York architects. When the elaborate plans reached her, she sent for a local contractor to estimate construction costs. Ben Muncil was a self-taught builder who already had a substantial reputation for creating several of the comfortable rustic camps on the St. Regis lakes. A summer resident of the lake, the Reverend W. B. Lusk, recalls the response of the untutored builder to Mrs. Post's request.

> Ben modestly pleaded that he hadn't even the education to read the plans or to give her anything like a reasonable idea of the cost; but, dropping the role of modesty, he ventured the opinion that such a camp as the drawings called for would be inappropriate in an Adirondack setting, and asked for an opportunity to submit a design of his own. One of her advisors, who happened to be present, intimated that Ben had not been summoned to give his opinion, or to offer a new design; upon which the lady herself said, Ben, prepare a drawing of the kind of camp that

Topridge's guest cottages of intersecting octagons and rectangles are perched along the main ridge. Shingled or slab-sided, the exteriors of the cottages were painted.

209

The rustic work of the Topridge boathouse merges with the surrounding forest. Used on structures, furniture, and decoration, tree roots, limbs, and trunks surround guests at the camp.

you think would be appropriate, and submit it to me at the earliest date you can! Within a week he had in her hands a rough sketch, details of which were elaborated and improved by her friend, Theodore Blake, an eminent architect, and within a month, Ben had commenced building operations that were to lead to the expenditure of over a half a million dollars in the erection of the Davies' camp, noted for its beauty of design and its perfect harmony with the Adirondack setting and surroundings.

Set on the crest of the ridge and hidden by dense foliage, the camp is almost invisible from the lake front. Only the boathouses, the landing for the funicular, and an occasional glimpse of the main lodge roof reveal the site. Most of the buildings are constructed of rough wood siding painted various shades of green or other bright colors. Mrs. Post preferred 'everything to be painted'; her favorite was white with red trim.

From the lake side, a visitor's first view of the camp is the boathouse, with its extraordinary detailing of roots, limbs, and twigs that surpasses any Durant invention. Functioning as a landing for guests, it also contains a second-story guest room. The progression from water's

Chandeliers of interwoven antlers light the living room of Topridge's main lodge.

edge to the main camp continues with a simpler structure that serves as the base landing of the funicular, a Muncil innovation.

At the top of the funicular is the main lodge, modestly rustic on the outside but with a splendidly opulent interior. Three times a week, guests and friends from the lake gathered here for meals, conversation, and full-length movies. The soaring space and richness of detail of the main living room is difficult to capture in photographs. From the entrance hall, one moves up treads formed by halved logs. Handrails fashioned of entire saplings curve gently and naturally to fit the stairway, and much larger trees, cut close to the base, form bannister posts. The living room, about eighty by one hundred feet, rises thirty feet to a ceiling supported by massive timbers. This is the room where films were shown — a 35mm projection room overlooks the space.

The room, still splendid, once contained a wealth of American Indian artifacts. Kayaks originally hanging from the ceiling have been removed to the Smithsonian Institution, along with an Indian basket collection. Baskets converted to light fixtures have been left as they are — suspended from the ceiling around the edges of the room.

The space is filled with animal artifacts as well. Two magnificent chandeliers of intertwined antlers hang over the center of the room. Bear and wolf skins rest on the floor, stuffed owls, possums, and foxes on the walls; pony hides and other pelts cover chairs and couches. At one end of the room is a huge stone fireplace flanked by benches. Hand-wrought andirons, fireplace enclosures, and other hardware are employed throughout. The adjacent dining room, which could seat thirty people, has a stucco ceiling ribbed with narrow logs.

Outside of the main-lodge kitchen is a screened porch with a large sink. Jim Bickford, Mrs. Post's last superintendent, remembers that it was used exclusively for the 'girls' to arrange fresh flowers, usually brought in from Washington by airplane.

Though the main lodge always had fine views of both Upper St. Regis Lake and Upper and Lower Spectacle ponds, Bickford relates that one day Mrs. Post entered the lodge and realized that the window was too small to allow a full view of St. Regis Mountain. She called one of her superintendents and instructed him to enlarge the window when she left in the fall. That fall the window opening was enlarged to ten and a half feet in height. A special piece of plate glass ordered from Utica was brought across St. Regis Lake by barge. It took fifteen men to install it, but Mrs. Post had her view. Several years later, an Air Force jet flying overhead created a sonic boom that broke the glass. The government reimbursed Mrs. Post to the tune of $3600 but the window was literally irreplaceable.

Upper St. Regis Lake framed by the Post boathouse bedroom porch.

*The Post
Dacha —
Adirondack
Made*

Other camp buildings are clustered around the main lodge on the narrow ridge. Two two-storied guest cottages, north of the main lodge facing St. Regis Lake, were available for those visitors who were not members of the family. Family cottages and other guest cottages were south of the main lodge. Clay tennis courts and putting greens were part of the elaborate grounds developed for the use of the family and guests.

At the south end of the camp complex is one of the camp's most interesting buildings. Completely at home in its Adirondack setting is a copy of a Russian dacha built for Joseph E. Davies, Mrs. Post's third husband, who was ambassador to the Soviet Union from 1936 to 1938. One of only a few log buildings at the camp, the structure is similar to one built on Mrs. Post's Washington, D.C. estate. Intricately carved and brightly decorated window frames and barge boards reveal the influence of Eastern Europe. The effect is sustained by a vaulted ceiling constructed of planks and trusses. One corner contains a tile stove, matched by a tiled fireplace at the other end of the room. Although on the surface a fine example of an imported dacha, the logs were cut, peeled, and notched by local craftsmen; decorative elements were fabricated in New York and shipped to the site. In later years, the building was used for square dances presided over by Mrs. Post. One evening after square dancing, she found that her coat, which she had hung on a hook outside the door, had become chilled. She called Bickford and told him to add a heated cloakroom by the following summer. Bickford said that she probably used the cloakroom only twice after that.

Among the largest of the Adirondack camps, Topridge is probably the most lavishly appointed, preserving an outward appearance of rusticity that belies its careful design.

A gift to the state of New York in 1974 from the Marjorie Merriweather Post Foundation, the camp is both endangered and controversial. The state does not pay property taxes to the town of Santa Clara, although it does make payments in lieu of taxes; still, expenditures on the camp are heavily criticized as a luxury in local and state presses. Temporarily safe from the 'forever wild' provision of the state constitution because it is operated by the New York State Office of General Services, the Great Camp is jeopardized by the lack of definitive public policy. The major concern about the camp is summed up in a statement made by Jim Bickford: 'No amount of use is worse than disuse.' Though a temporary solution was provided recently by cutting a road into the site and winterizing buildings for guests at the 1980 Lake Placid Olympic Winter Games, and though plans for opening the camp for conferences and group visits will provide some income to offset operating costs, until a definitive policy is set by the state, the camp's future is uncertain.

Above and below left,
*dacha at Topridge,
built by local crafts-
men.* Below right, *a
Russian-tiled fireplace
decorates a corner of
Topridge's dacha.*

Minnowbrook:
The Last of
the Great
Camps

THE HERITAGE OF William West Durant's originality was carried on by a succession of camp owners who maintained his ideals by building in a manner responsive to the natural environment. For over a century they have been aided and abetted by a remarkably responsive craft tradition. They have been guided, moreover, by a group of architects who have embraced that tradition and often extended it. Wareham and DeLair, the successors to an architectural firm founded in Saranac Lake Village in the 1890s, provide an unbroken chain from the work of Durant to the present that is expressed in the last of the Great Camps, Minnowbrook, built at Blue Mountain Lake in 1948 and 1949.

William Coulter established his architectural practice in 1895. His early rustic cottage designs attracted several Great Camp owners as clients. Max Westhoff joined him in the early 1900s for a brief period; William Distin became a partner around 1911 and carried on the firm for the next four decades until he was joined by Arthur Wareham. The firm of Wareham & DeLair now continues the practice. Little of the

Opposite, *the main lodge of Camp Minnowbrook, from Blue Mountain Lake.* Above, *Coulter's massive main lodge completes the transition from delicate tent platforms. The central chalet-like form connects the lower sleeping and service wings.* Left, *the octagonal woodshed at Minnowbrook illustrates the need for massive framing to withstand an Adirondack snowfall.*

personal history of the early principals is recorded, but the architectural work of the firm recapitulates the history of the Great Camps from Durant to the present.

There are probably other camps that can vie for the title of 'last,' but Minnowbrook's claim is underscored by its site and its builder; it is built on part of Durant's Forest Park and Land Company holdings and was designed by William Distin. Following Coulter's basic style, Distin brought Durant's rustic approach to lodge construction up to date.

The Minnowbrook property was the site of a hunting lodge and several service buildings when it was acquired by the R. M. Hollingshead Corporation in 1944. After a fire destroyed the main lodge in late 1947, Distin began planning the new camp. By 1949 the main lodge, a guest house, boathouse, and several support buildings were completed. Hollingshead used the camp through 1953 when it was donated to Syracuse University for use as a conference center. Although buildings have been added over the years to expand sleeping capacity, and modest alterations made to simplify maintenance, the camp retains its original spirit, contours, and integrity.

One of the early buildings was an airplane hangar built on the lakeshore in 1946 to accommodate the Hollingshead Company planes. A submerged ramp was connected directly to the building. After the fire destroyed the original lodge, a guest house was built to house construction crews. To this was attached a greenhouse, and nearby an icehouse was erected. A dramatic ten-sided woodshed of open framing was also built to service the camp.

In planning the main lodge, Distin emphasized the traditional Swiss characteristics but gave his design modern touches, especially in his use of massive features. Informal and relaxed, the main lodge deliberately refuses to conform to the rigid demands for balance imposed on older Adirondack lodges. Distin did retain Durant's notion that a building should blend perfectly with its environment: the site for the lodge was carefully selected on a ridge above the lake and commands magnificent views to the west, south, and east. The ground-floor plan of the lodge follows the curve of the ridge, extending two hundred feet from end to end. Intersecting hip roofs cover the rambling one-story wings and the two-story central portion. Although rustic in overall appearance — with exterior log siding, shingled roof, and many skillfully executed interior log details — the main lodge and guest cabin are wood-frame structures on concrete foundations.

Indigenous stone was secured for the exterior chimneys, but the type of wood necessary for permanent exterior siding could no longer be found locally. Logs of British Columbia red cedar and western Canadian jack pine were finally located in a Montreal lumber yard. These logs, ordinarily used for telephone poles, were sent to Minnowbrook where they were cut into proper lengths. Oregon cedar logs, naturally water resistant, were sent from the West Coast to be cut on site into roof shingling.

The planning of the main lodge represents the maturity of Great Camp design. A living room of grand proportions is flanked on one side by a sleeping wing of five bedrooms and on the other side by a wing containing social rooms, dining room, and kitchen. Interiors display rustic details, fine design, and excellent workmanship in a variety of woods. A woodworking shop was set up on the site, and all sash and doors were made there, as well as much of the furniture. Wrought-iron light fixtures and hardware were made by a local smith to the architect's specifications.

The social spaces in particular were given extraordinary attention in detail and execution. A library is paneled in mahogany taken from a Philadelphia townhouse. The bar has walls and ceilings sheathed with weathered boards from an 85-year-old barn near Saranac Lake. Thinking that a crooked chimney would add authenticity to the room, Hollingshead told the stone masons what he wanted. Three times the task was completed and each time the owner found a perfectly straight chimney. After the masons were required to rebuild it several times, they became so irritated that they practically threw the bricks into the mortar — achieving exactly the desired results in the process.

Through a chain of coincidences, possessions of William West Durant are now in use at Minnowbrook. After a day of wandering through the lands first assembled by Durant and enjoying the magnificent setting of woods and water, the modern visitor can return to a Great Camp replete with the earliest rustic traditions, and to the comfort of a bed covered with blankets of scarlet red and black stripes bearing the monogram 'w.w.d.'

The history of the camp and its present use illustrate much of the past, present, and future of the Great Camps. That a private educational institution has continued to use the camp, keeping much of its original character intact, proves that a concerned owner and a conscientious caretaker are essential to the preservation of a Great Camp.

So much for the description of these ten Great Camps; all in one way or another constitute parts of Durant's legacy. But the haunting question remains — how many of those still standing will survive and how many will be razed, their sites returned to nature?

Opposite, *the unavailability of local logs required use of Western Canada firs previously meant for telephone poles. At Minnowbrook they are used sparingly as a veneer for siding with the end joints giving the appearance of solid log construction.* Left, *Minnowbrook's log detailing in the Durant tradition.* Below, *Blue Mountain Lake on a spring morning.*

CHAPTER 10

THE FUTURE
OF THE GREAT CAMPS

Footbridge extending out into Upper Saranac Lake from Seligman's Sekon Lodge

SCENT OF PINE. Wind-ruffled water lapping a shore in the summer sun. The cry of a loon skimming a forest-edged lake. Flash of white birch, of doe and deer. Leaf blaze in autumn. Crack of freezing trees splitting the winter silence. A line of buckets hooked to maples in sap time. The muddy miracle of March. Images of the Adirondacks. As nature turns and turns again in its beauteous round, so man, where he has withheld his rapacity and built in harmony with nature, has left a precious heritage, now part of that beauty.

Across millions of forested acres and in the brief span of fifty years, families of great wealth came to get away from it all — in style. The camps they built express a twofold architectural achievement — harmony with nature and triumph over it. The delicately placed rustic work of twigs and branches set into spruce bark at Raquette Lake has survived a century of winters. In strong contrast are the refined cottages of Upper St. Regis Lake and the massive log hunting lodges of Saranac. On populous lakeshores or deep in private preserves of tens of thousands of acres, the family retreats of the wealthy form the special architectural and cultural legacies of the Adirondacks.

Slowly and sometimes dramatically the Great Camps are being lost. Neglect by inheritors of the Morgan, Huntington, and Vanderbilt estates is evident. Severe Adirondack winters take their toll, and sale to those with immediate commercial interests has resulted in alterations, reckless subdivision of property, and even destruction to clear land for new buildings. A sense of stewardship and love for the camps war with constantly increasing costs. As a result, each year decisions are reluctantly made by heirs or trustees, sealing the fate of one camp after another forever.

To preserve the camps is not to make remote museums of former playgrounds of the rich but to save unique structures embodying a regionally distinct architectural tradition. More than this, the camps are living lessons that have much to teach: how to build in harmony with nature, how to use local materials and craft traditions — in short, how to live in nature without destroying it. The camps are architectural treasures that, once lost, can never be replaced.

The Problem of the Camps

THE PRESERVATION of the Great Camps is difficult. Harold Hochschild summed up the changes in lifestyles and social attitudes that have created the problem of the camps: 'their era has passed its zenith.' The period of camp building was short, covering fifty years from 1880 to 1930. The opening of the region by railroads and society's 'discovery' stirred great interest at the turn of the century, but the era ended with the Depression. Abandoning, selling, or demolishing began then, accelerating after World War II.

Echo Camp, Raquette Lake.

Several important changes have contributed to this process. The isolation of the camps, hence their need for self-sufficiency, required sizable year-round staffs to maintain the family quarters, grounds, and outbuildings to serve camp residents and guests. Rising costs of labor and maintenance — and a reduced number of people willing to work in this role — have added to camp owners' burdens. The camps, once showcases of wealth and power, have become too expensive to operate and repair today.

Technology and economics have also affected fashions in social life. The large, upperclass family with several generations vacationing together has become the exception not the rule, leaving to oblivion the staff necessary to service it. Families now are smaller, and members follow the seasons by jet. The old estates, little more than white elephants, are left behind for easy-care condominiums in the Rockies or Alps, the Caribbean or Mediterranean. The devastating effect of acid rains on the fish life in the high Adirondack lakes, coupled with an invasion of the *hoi polloi*, eliminate the traditional pleasures and attractions for wealthy camp owners.

Income, inheritance, and property taxes have also hit the camp owners hard. It is increasingly difficult to simultaneously pay inheritance taxes, satisfy the demands of growing numbers of heirs, and maintain a large property intact. With a fragile economic base at best, Adirondack towns and counties are sorely pressed for tax revenues. These Great Camps, with their vast holdings, tempt residents to raise property taxes — especially for 'outsiders' — to support local social programs. Even of those who can afford to pay the taxes more and more refuse to saddle themselves with unwieldy properties, however much they cherish them.

Owners of camps have coped with these pressures in a variety of ways. Some have cut back on staff and maintenance. An honorable approach, and one with tax advantages, has been to donate the property to religious, educational, or other nonprofit organizations. In recent years, this solution has become increasingly difficult, for even these institutions are less and less able to meet costs of upkeep and operation. For example, costs of maintenance and declining revenues forced Syracuse University to sell off Sagamore and Camp Pinebrook on Upper Saranac Lake; and the Boy Scouts of Bergen County, New Jersey, can no longer afford travel to Camp Uncas.

The other solution has been to sell part or all of the property to the state of New York or to other private owners, often for subdivision. Subdividing the land can threaten the character of a camp itself, as occurred at Sekon Lodge on Upper Saranac Lake, while sale to the state raises the possibility of the destruction of buildings by enforcement of 'forever wild' provisions of the state constitution. In 1952 Harold Hochschild summarized the problem of preserving the Great Camps: 'The lack of a new class of buyers leaves the fate of these private camps in doubt. In the course of time they are likely to pass into the hands of public agencies or institutions or to be sold for their scrap value.'

Because of the large land holdings, the preserves are an essential part of whatever future the wilderness has in the Adirondack Park. Today, at least a dozen preserves of 5000 acres or more contain complexes of buildings representing the finest examples of Great Camps, now either in the hands of the state or potentially available for acquisition. Remote from traveled routes, their construction and sustenance is and was more than just difficult (even in the nineteenth century, a visitor to Kamp Kill Kare had to make two changes of railroads and a twenty-five-mile buckboard or sleigh ride to reach the camp).

Clearly, these traditional solutions to ensure the survival of the Great Camps are no longer viable. Nor are methods that were used elsewhere to save historic buildings and sites, for these do not fit the Adirondack conditions.

*The Camp
Owner's
Dilemma*

Utility and Enjoyment

ALMOST A CENTURY and a half ago the writers and artists who discovered the joys of the Adirondacks began to bring back tales and sketches that fascinated city dwellers of a burgeoning America. Westward expansion had left large tracts of heavily forested and largely uninhabited mountainous country in northern New York that were described as an 'enchanted island' where those in quest of health and refreshment could find relief from 'the busy world away from its noise and tumult, its cares and perplexities.' The region also drew those interested in exploiting the rich potential of its forests and underground minerals. In due course the rush of tourists, land speculators, and lumbermen focused concern on the erosion of the Adirondack wilderness.

'Utility and enjoyment' is how a *New York Times* editorial in 1864 framed the argument: could a natural landscape such as the Adirondacks be developed for economic benefit and not have its scenic

Hale's Camp, Ausable Club.

beauty despoiled? Ninety years later, William Chapman White in his homage to the region — *Adirondack Country* — chose as his two themes 'the ever widening use of the region as a vacation area' and the conflicting 'acute problems that have arisen in considering the future of the woods.'

Ever since, the debate has raged between those who would give priority to economic development and those for whom such development had to be made compatible with conservation.

Braided into the double strand of these two is the issue of architectural preservation. Environmentalists have opposed preservationists here, sometimes finding themselves allied with development interests.

*Swiss chalet influence:
the Hamlin House at
Lake Placid.*

These odd bedfellows now find themselves arguing for the same policies that in other regions have kept them in determined opposition.

Environmental conservation became a public question as early as the mid-nineteenth century. Men like James Fenimore Cooper and Henry David Thoreau began to realize the destructive potential of unchecked economic exploitation and established the terms of the argument for conservation.

Preservation of architecture did not gain momentum as a movement until a century later, when neglect or destruction under the guise of progress aroused determined individuals to preserve early examples of the nation's buildings. The movement now underway for architectural preservation establishing the legal basis necessary for protection of such structures is similar to wilderness protection in motivation — the maintenance of connections with America's past.

Saving historic buildings in areas of natural beauty, however, is not an issue common enough to have established precedents. The Adirondacks present complications that, if resolved in favor of the Great Camps, will establish principles of conservation and preservation elsewhere. In a setting where enlightened environmental protection has existed since 1894, preceding the National Wilderness Act of 1964 by seventy years, a tradition of benign public interest favors reasonable accommodation of all parties.

The history of the creation of the Adirondack Park is an important element in understanding the conflict emerging between nineteenth-century preservationists and expansionists. As early as the 1850s Samuel H. Hammond outlined the concept of limited wild areas within 'a circle of a hundred miles in diameter protected by the constitution' as a means of conserving, without gainsaying development. By the end of the century, more had been written about the Adirondack country than any other wilderness area in the United States. As the urban population of the Eastern United States increased and more people crowded into the cities, the Adirondacks received still more attention. One anonymous writer, describing the region's charms, sadly concluded that 'in a few years, the railroad with its iron web will bind the free forest, the lakes will lose their solitude, the deer and moose will flee to a safer resort . . . and men with axe and spade will work out a revolution.'

The controversy over conservation and development that created the Adirondack Park produced arguments still being debated today. What has changed, however, is not the nature of the debate but the cast of characters who conduct it. Now armed with a more enlightened self-interest, the giant lumber companies have become leaders in conservation, their old exploitive role assumed by others seeking rapid return on inevitably irresponsible development. While the natives of the area legitimately seek opportunities for employment in this chronically depressed area, the land speculator seeks profitable development for recreation purposes, whatever the cost to the remaining wilderness. Pitted against these groups are the conservationists, characterized as owners of second homes and 'outsiders,' although often numbering among them are natives attempting to preserve the area's natural beauty.

Moreover, the small, permanent population is diffused throughout millions of acres of wilderness, making community organizing on a regional scale difficult. Several groups made up of natives and 'outsiders' are actively concerned, but even residents may not know when a Great

Camp is threatened, and others outside the region may not even know it exists.

Administration and management on the state land is complicated by the presence of three agencies with overlapping responsibilities. The Department of Environmental Conservation and the Office of Parks and Recreation have traditions of protecting the environment and improving public access to the region. To these two has recently been added a land-use coordinating Adirondack Park Agency. Exacerbating the situation are the constituencies of these organizations, each with their own priorities and their own systems of pressure.

The glamorous social life of the Great Camps has tended to receive more attention than its architecture. However, the preservation of the Great Camps is not a matter of memorializing affluent citizens of the past. Confrontations between wilderness advocates and those who would save structures of historic and architectural significance in the Adirondacks are likely to presage similar fights elsewhere — in the 'gold coasts' outside cities like New York, Boston, Detroit, and Chicago — where grand estates have the potential to be converted to nature preserves. Solutions achieved here can set the same kind of salutary precedent as those that created the Adirondack Forest Preserve and Park in the first place.

Gerster's Cabin at Bennett's Hotel, Raquette Lake.

Preservation of the Camps

TO MANY PEOPLE, the words 'historic preservation' have an elitist ring, conjuring up images of well-meaning dowagers engaged in a white-glove cause. Until recently, historic preservation has been little more than that. Public interest in enshrining historical sites emerged in this country after the Civil War when well-to-do ladies and gentlemen raised funds to obtain and restore a Mount Vernon or a Gettysburg, turning them into museums or parks. Over the years, the notion of historic preservation has gone beyond this preoccupation.

Topridge,
St. Regis Lake.

Processes for preservation of the Great Camps are more complex than those necessary to save an endangered urban building or site from the developer. The first steps to solutions have been agreed on: comprehensive inventory; a constitutional amendment if required; land acquisition; the identification and development of suitable adaptive uses; and the reform of real-property tax provisions. In the process of preservation, it is essential that polarization of interests be avoided. 'Forever wilders' may react defensively towards architectural-preservation proposals not judiciously framed in terms of the same historical-preservation instinct that informs the urge to preserve the wilderness.

The fate of all the remaining thirty-five Great Camps is precarious. Camps well cared for now in private or institutional hands are subject to sudden changes in family situation or to equally pressing economic decisions thrust on nonprofit organization trustees. Santanoni and

Topridge are owned by the state of New York but face uncertain futures. The grouping of Sagamore, Uncas, and Kill Kare is of such historic importance that present private owners should be supported in their stewardship. Other private preserves surrounded by vast acreage should be protected before, like Nehasane, they face demolition under the 'forever wild' stipulation. The question, and it is a public question, is how such support and protection is to be provided.

Many ideas, similar to those for preserving large estates in environments other than the Adirondacks, have been put forward. Creative solutions require tax relief for the owners; provision for reasonable fees for the owners or heirs if public access is permitted; and guarantees to preserve the character and architectural integrity of a camp in the event of a private sale or assumptions of ownership by the state.

Some observers believe an administrative method can be used to protect the Great Camps: the state could declare them educational resources, a move that might spare them from demolition, and avoid the uncertain.

Regional land-use planning is one of the most effective tools available for the protection and preservation of the Adirondacks without unduly impeding their growth and economic development. The Adirondack Park Agency has the legislative mandate to channel development and to regulate the use of the natural resources. With its thorough knowledge of the natural, political, sociological, and economic characteristics of the area, and through cooperative ventures with the Department of Environmental Conservation and the Office of Parks and Recreation, the Agency can act to save some of the camps for future public use.

Not all the camps can be preserved, but the finest or most exemplary are worthy of public action.[*] The state would do well to consider the potential of the Great Camps to house, educate, and entertain the increasing number of wilderness visitors. To demolish any of the Great Camps only to replace them with institutional, modern structures would be a foolish waste — of heritage, material, time, and money.

The mountain season for tourism has been traditionally quite short — ten to fifteen weeks, from early July to early October. But in recent years development of winter sports has offered new hope to the sagging economy. In the Fulton Chain and Gore Mountain areas, winter income derived from ski-mobilers and downhill and cross-country skiers on trails developed by the state and local governments, now exceeds summer income for some businesses. The Olympic Winter

*Creative
Solutions
for Camp
Preservation*

---

[*] Unpublished survey material for approximately forty Adirondack Great Camps is available for inspection at the Preservation League's office in Albany, New York.

*Permanent 'tents'
at Nehasane.*

Games at Lake Placid in 1980 attracted world-wide attention, and re-opened the Adirondack Railroad from Utica to Lake Placid. Train travel may make year-round outings to the central Adirondacks fashionable again as private automobile travel becomes more and more expensive.

A circuit of Great Camps made accessible to the public, similar to the missions of San Antonio or the country estates of Britain, would be a significant tourist attraction. The annual increase of visitors to properties of the National Trust for Historic Preservation encourages this adaptive reuse of Great Camps. If a network of guest houses, conference centers, hostels, or similar public facilities were established to make use of the Great Camps, travel throughout the region would be encouraged. Imagine the attractiveness of a vacation spent with a day or so at each successive Great Camp!

Genuine economies in the maintenance of the Great Camps are possible — through shared overhead of administration, insurance, promotion, and operational costs — if a chain of camps were organized as public facilities. A year-round maintenance crew, for example, might travel around the circuit or be available on call. A central reservation service could direct visitors to available accommodations.

How the woods should be used, by whom, and on what terms has been a sensitive and often controversial question. Adaptive use could sustain the Great Camps, widely scattered throughout the vast region, without instituting a major policy change affecting all of the public land. Conferences or campers have hardly disturbed the natural qualities of Sagamore, Minnowbrook, Pine Knot, Echo Camp, or Lewisohn's Prospect Point Camp over the past decades. Adaptive use should not be seen as a threat to the wilderness, therefore, but as a provision for its greater appreciation, thus deepening the commitment to protect it.

Conclusion

THE LONG TRADITION of land stewardship, wise state land legislation, and hosts of individual decisions made by those who cherish the Adirondacks have carried their treasures into the present — a tradition sustaining the conviction that the Great Camps can be preserved. In 1902 W.H.H. 'Adirondack' Murray, surveying the Park his *Adventures in the Wilderness* helped create, made plain that New York does not own the Adirondacks, but 'holds them in trust for the people. They stand for forces that affect the mind, body and soul of men to . . . a degree so salutary [that] they are lifted above the monetary classment.'

The trust Murray defined and personified bequeaths a stewardship to us all. Unless enlightened public opinion and a creative public service invent a way to save the Great Camps, it is all too clear that we shall live to see their destruction.

Raquette Lake

BIBLIOGRAPHY

Aber, Ted, and King, Stella, *The History of Hamilton County*. Lake Pleasant, N.Y.: Great Wilderness Books, 1965.

'Adirondack,' Editorial. *New York Times*, August 9, 1864.

Adirondack Bibliography: A List of Books, Pamphlets and Periodical Articles published through the year 1955. Gabriels, N.Y.: Adirondack Mountain Club, 1958.

————. Supplement, 1956–65. Compiled by the Bibliography Committee, Adirondack Mountain Club. Blue Mountain Lake, N.Y.: The Adirondack Museum, 1973.

'Adirondack Camps.' *Forest and Stream* (May 30, 1908), 70:847.

'An Adirondack Lodge.' *House and Garden* (Dec. 1907), 12:203–207.

'An Adirondack Lodge for William A. Read.' *American Architect and Building News* (July 14, 1906), p. 90.

'Adirondack Private Preserves.' *Eighth Annual Report of the Forest, Fish and Game Commission of New York State*. Albany: Wyncoop, Hallenbeck and Crawford Co., 1903. pp. 37–44 (For year ending September 30, 1902).

Amory, Cleveland. *The Last Resorts*. New York: Harper and Brothers, 1948.

Annual Report of the Forest Commission of New York State. 9 Vols. Albany: The Argus Company, James B. Lyon (etc.), 1886–1895.

Applegate, Howard Lewis. *The Story of Minnowbrook*. Series of Papers on Adult Education, No. 27. Syracuse, N.Y.: University College of Syracuse University, 1962.

————. *The Story of Pinebrook*. Series of Papers on Adult Education, No. 19. Syracuse, N.Y.: University College of Syracuse University, 1962.

————. *The Story of Sagamore*. Series of Papers on Adult Education, No. 19, Syracuse, N.Y.: University College of Syracuse University, 1962.

Arthur, Eric and Witney, Dudley. *The Barn: A Vanishing Landmark in North America*. Toronto: McClelland and Stewart, 1972.

Birmingham, Stephen. *Our Crowd*. New York: Harper and Row, 1967.

————. *The Right People*. Boston: Little, Brown & Co., 1958.

Brimmer, Frank Everett. *Camps, Log Cabins, Lodges and Clubhouses*. New York: D. Appleton, 1925.

Bruette, William A. *Log Camps and Cabins*. New York: The Nessmunk Library, 1934.

Collins, Geraldine. *The Brighton Story*. Lakemont, N.Y.: North Country Books, 1977.

Colvin, Verplanck. *Seventh Annual Report of the Topographical Survey of the Adirondack Region of New York (1874–1879)*. Albany: Weed, Parson and Company, 1880.

Dana, William S. B. *The Swiss Chalet Book*. New York: William T. Comstock Co., 1913.

DeSormo, Maitland D. *The Heydays of the Adirondacks*. Saranac Lake, N.Y.: Adirondack Yesteryears, Inc., 1974.

————. *Seneca Ray Stoddard*. Saranac Lake, N.Y.: Adirondack Yesteryears, Inc., 1972.

————. *Summers on the Adirondacks*. Saranac Lake, N.Y.: Adirondack Yesteryears, Inc., 1980.

Dix, William Frederick. 'Summer Life in Luxurious Adirondack Camps.' *The Independent* (July 2, 1903), 1556–1562.

Doctorow, E. A. *Loon Lake*. New York: Random House, 1980.

Donaldson, Alfred L. *A History of the Adirondacks*. 2 vols. New York: The Century Company, 1921.

Downing, Andrew Jackson. *The Architecture of Country Houses*. Boston: Appleton and Co., 1950.

————. *Cottage Residences*. New York: Wiley and Putnam, 1844.

Encyclopedia of American Biography. New Series, New York: American Historical Society, 1935.

Flexner, James Thomas. *That Wilder Image*. Boston: Little, Brown and Company, 1962.

Gadski, Mary Ellen Donblewski. *Research Report on the Great Camps of the Adirondacks*. Albany: The Preservation League of New York State, June 1978.

Gonino, Vincent J. *The Story of the Huntington Memorial Camp*. Dubuque, Iowa: Kendall/Hunt Publishing Company, 1974.

Graham, Frank, Jr. *The Adirondack Park*. New York: Alfred A. Knopf, 1978.

Gropius, Walter. *Katsura: Tradition and Creation in Japanese Architecture*. New Haven: Yale University Press, 1960.

Hammond, Samuel H. *Wild Northern Scenes*. New York: Derby and Jackson, 1857.

Headley, Joel T. *The Adirondack: or Life in the Woods*. New York: Scribner, Armstrong and Company, 1849.

Hochschild, Harold K. *Township 34*. New York: Published by the Author, 1952.

Hoffman, Charles Fenno. *Wild Scenes in the Forest and Prairies*. London: Richard Bentley, 1839.

Hooker, Mildred Phelps Stokes. *Camp Chronicles*. Blue Mountain Lake, N.Y.: Adirondack Museum, 1964.

Hough, Franklin B. *A History of St. Lawrence and Franklin Counties, New York from the Earliest Times*. Albany: Little & Co., 1853.

Hoyt, Edwin P. *The Vanderbilts and Their Fortunes*. Garden City, N.Y.: Doubleday and Company, 1902.

Ives, Martin V. B. *Through the Adirondacks in Eighteen Days*. New York and Albany: Wyncoop, Hallenbeck and Crawford Co., 1899.

Jacquet, Pierre. *Le Chalet Suisse*. Zurich: Orell Füssli Verlag, 1963.

Jordan, Terry G. *Texas Log Buildings, A Folk Architecture*. Austin: University of Texas Press, 1977.

Keller, Jane E. *Adirondack Wilderness*. Syracuse, N.Y.: Syracuse University Press, 1980.

Kellogg, Alice M. 'Luxurious Adirondack Camps.' *New Broadway Magazine* (August 1908), 21:207–212.

Kelly, Allen. 'An Adirondack Park.' *Harper's Weekly* (July 19, 1890), 34:563.

Kniffen, Fred and Glassie, Henry. 'Building in Wood in the Eastern United States.' *Geographical Review* (1966), 56:40–66.

Lancaster, Clay. *The Japanese Influence in America*. New York: Walton H. Rawls, 1963.

Langdon, Philip. 'Compromise with Nature.' *Historic Preservation* (September/October 1979), 31:13–21.

Lehman, Arnold. *Great Camps of the Adirondacks: A Wilderness Architecture*. Albany, New York: Adirondack Museum Library. Ms. 73–11.

Longstreth, T. Morris. *The Adirondacks*. New York: Century Company, 1917.

McArdle, Alma C. and Deirdre B. *Carpenter Gothic.* New York: Whitney Library of Design, 1978.

McGowan, Robert Harold. *Architecture from the Adirondack Foothills.* Malone, N.Y.: Franklin County Historical and Museum Society, 1977.

McQueen, Peter and Smith, J. Hyatt. 'Life in the Adirondacks.' *Munsey's Magazine* (February, 1893), 8:479–493.

Mackinson, Randell L. *Greene and Greene: Architecture as a Fine Art.* Salt Lake City: Peregrine Smith, Inc., 1977.

Malo, Paul. 'The Great Camps of the Adirondacks.' *Saving Large Estates*, pp. 173–178. Ed. by William C. Shopsin and Grania Bolton Marcus. Setauket, N.Y.: Society for the Preservation of Long Island Antiquities, 1977.

Masten, Arthur H. *The Story of Adirondack.* Syracuse, N.Y.: Syracuse University Press, 1968.

Mercer, Henry. *The Origin of Log Houses in the United States.* Doylestown, Pa.: Bucks County Historical Association, 1924.

Murray, William H. H. *Adventures in the Wilderness; or Camp Life in the Adirondacks.* Boston: Fields, Osgood, and Company, 1869.

'A Millionaire's Camp in the Adirondacks.' *Keith's Magazine* (July, 1913), 30:31–33.

Nash, Roderick. *Wilderness and the American Mind.* Revised ed. New Haven: Yale University Press, 1973.

Osgood, J. 'Picknicking in the Adirondacks.' *Outing* (July, 1889), 14:284–288.

Palliser's New Cottage Home and Details. New York: Palliser, Palliser and Company, 1887.

Platt, Frederick. *America's Gilded Age.* Cranbury, N.Y.: A. S. Barnes and Company, 1976.

Plumb, Barbara. 'How the Morgans Roughed It.' *New York Times Magazine* (August 21, 1966), 74–80.

'Private Preserves in the Adirondack Forests.' *Annual Report of the Forest Commission of New York State for the Year 1893.* Albany: James B. Lyon, 1894. 1: 151–201.

Post, Emily. *Etiquette.* Chap XXVI, pp. 440–447. New York: Funk and Wagnall's Co., 1922.

Reznikoff, Charles. *Louis Marshall: Champion of Liberty.* Phila.: The Jewish Publication Society of America, 1957.

Roth, Leland M. *The Architecture of McKim, Mead and White, 1870–1920. A Building List.* New York: Garland Publishing Company, 1978.

Saylor, Henry H. *Bungalows.* New York: Robert H. McBride & Co., 1926.

Scully, Vincent J., Jr. *The Shingle Style.* New Haven: Yale University Press, 1955.

Seaver, Franklin. *Historical Sketches of Franklin County.* Albany: G. B. Lyon, 1918.

Seton, Grace Gallatin. 'The Luxury of American Camping Life.' *The Delineator* (August, 1909), 74: 116–117, 150.

Shepard, Augustus D. *Camps in the Woods.* New York: New York Architectural Book Publishing Company, Inc., 1931.

Shopsin, William Cand Marcus. *Saving Large Estates.* Ed. by Grania Bolton. Setauket, N.Y.: Society for the Preservation of Long Island Antiquities, 1977.

Shurtleff, Harold R. *The Log Cabin Myth.* Cambridge: Harvard University Press, 1939.

Stoddard, Seneca Ray. *The Adirondacks Illustrated.* Glens Falls, N.Y.: Published by the Author (Editions from 1874 to 1917).

————. 'Map of the Adirondack Wilderness.' 18th rev. ed. New York: Louis E. Meuman and Co., 1895.

'Summer Homes in the Adirondacks.' *Mail and Express Illustrated Saturday Magazine* (August 16, 1902), 8–9.

'Types of Woodland Camps.' *Town and Country* (August 22, 1908), 12–13.

Verner, William K. 'Art and the Adirondacks.' *Antiques* (July, 1971), 100: 85–92.

————. 'Wilderness and the Adirondacks — An Historical View.' *The Living Wilderness* (Winter, 1969), 33:27.

Viollet-Le-Duc, Eugene. *The Habitations of Man in All Ages*. London: Sampson, Low, 1876.

Wack, Henry Wellington. 'Kamp Kill Kare: The Adirondack Home of the Honorable Timothy L. Woodruff.' *Field and Stream* (February, 1903), 7: 651–661.

Wallace, Edwin R. *Descriptive Guide to the Adirondacks*. Syracuse: Waverly Publishing Company, 1875.

————. *Guide to the Adirondacks*. Syracuse: W. Gill, 1894.

Weslager, Clinton A. *The Log Cabin in America*. New Brunswick, N.J.: Rutgers University Press, 1969.

Whipple, James S. 'Trip to Camp Kill-Kare.' *Albany Argus* (March 12, 1899), 14.

White, William Chapman. *Adirondack Country*. New York: Alfred A. Knopf, 1977.

Whitton, L. C. 'The Saint Regis Camps.' *Forest and Stream* (June 18, 1891), 36:435.

Wicks, William S. *Log Cabins: How to Build and Furnish Them*. New York: Forest and Stream Publishing Company, 1889.

Withey, Henry F. and Elsie R. *Biographical Dictionary of American Architects. (Deceased)*. Los Angeles: New Age Publishing Company, 1956.

Wodehouse, Lawrence. *American Architects from the Civil War to the First World War*. Detroit: Gale Research Company, 1976.

Woodward, George E. *Woodward's Country Homes*. New York: George E. Woodward Company, 1868.

Wright, William. *Heiress: The Rich Life of Marjorie Merriweather Post*. Washington: New Republic Books, 1978.

GREAT CAMPS OF THE ADIRONDACKS

has been designed by Frank J. Lieberman and set by American Book–Stratford Press, Inc., Saddle Brook, New Jersey, in Bodoni Book, a face named after Giambattista Bodoni (1740–1813), the son of a Piedmontese printer. After gaining renown and experience as superintendent of the Press of Propaganda in Rome, Bodoni became head of the ducal printing house of Parma in 1768. A great innovator in type design, his faces are known for their openness and delicacy.

The display type has been set by Solotype Designers and Typographers, Oakland, California.

The separations, printing, and binding were supervised by Chanticleer Press, New York, New York.

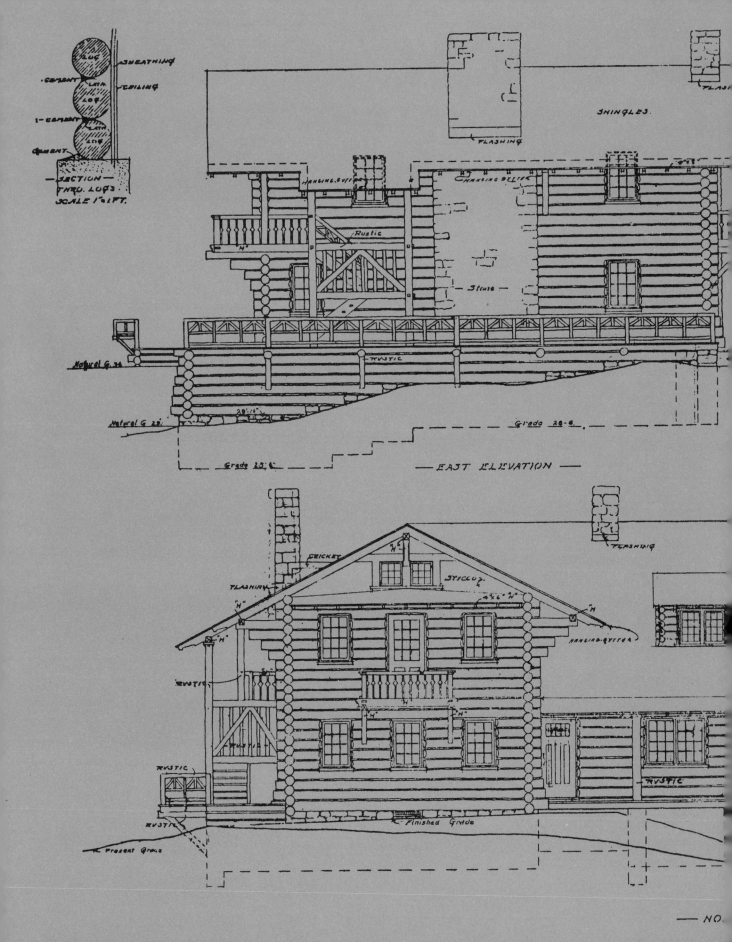

— EAST ELEVATION —

— NO.

ADIRONDACK LODG

Davis, McGr

The American Architect and Building News.
Regular Edition.

Copyright, 1906,